NINJA Speedi On a Budg£t

Simple, budget friendly and comforting recipes to save time, energy and money.

Helen Charles

BALVAIRD
— PUBLISHING —

Balvaird Publishing LLC
30 N Gould St Ste 32278
Sheridan, WY 82801

Author: Helen Charles
Editor: Hanley Knight
Illustrator: Glen Franklin

ISBN 978-1-960797-18-6 (Paperback).
ISBN 978-1-960797-11-7 (eBook).

Introduction

Hello, I'm Helen. I've always believed that cooking on a budget doesn't have to be challenging and it doesn't have to mean sacrificing flavour. Cooking on a budget does not have to mean cheese on toast every night for supper (although I do enjoy a cheesy toastie and think that it is a fantastic cheap supper!). In fact, some of the most delicious, satisfying and flavorful meals can be made with simple, cheap ingredients.

In this recipe book you'll find tips for cooking on a budget without reducing the quality of your food. you'll also find a collection of mouthwatering and simple-to-make recipes that will not splash the cash. These recipes include everything from breakfast to supper as well as desserts and sides.

So let's get cooking, and start saving!

Helen Charles

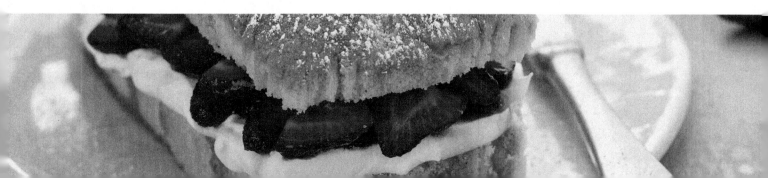

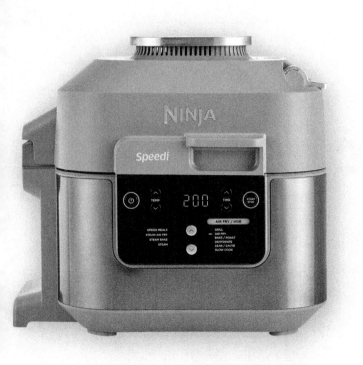

Ninja Speedi Guide

PLENTY OF FUNCTIONS AND QUICK MEALS IN ONE POT.

The Ninja Speedi is an excellent kitchen appliance. This multi-cooker is simple to use and can cook two different dishes, using two different cooking functions, at the same time. In less than 15 minutes .

SAY BYE-BYE TO YOUR OVEN

Ninja Speedi heats up quickly and cooks faster than your oven, thereby it uses far less energy, meaning it saves you cash on bills.

ONE SINGLE LID

The Ninja Speedi has a single lid, making it easier to use multiple functions without having to swap between lids.

The SmartSwitch

The **SmartSwitch** allows you to switch between the Rapid Cooker and Air Fry/Hob modes with ease.

You can choose between two modes:
1. *RAPID COOKER* mode or,
2. *AIR FRY / HOB* mode.

RAPID COOKER

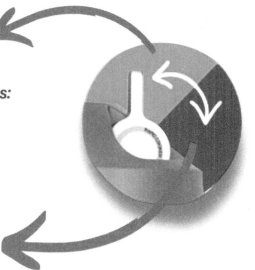

The Rapid Cooker mode has 4 cooking functions:
- Speedi Meals
- Steam Air Fry
- Steam Bake
- Steam

AIR FRY / HOB

The AIR FRY / HOB mode has 6 cooking functions:
- Grill
- Air Fry
- Bake/Roast
- Dehydrate
- Sear/Sauté
- Slow Cook

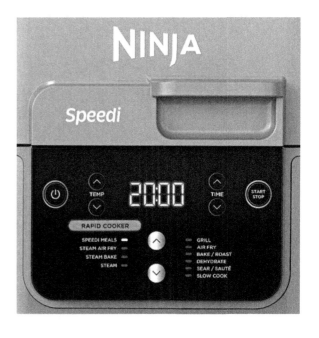

Cooking On a Budget

Budget-friendly cooking involves being aware of your spending when buying groceries, planning meals ahead, and making smart decisions. Below you'll find some useful tips to help you shop smart and make a good use of your fridge, freezer and cupboard.

Here are the best Budget Friendly Groceries Shopping Tips :

Check your fridge, freezer, and cupboard

Before you go shopping, make a list of what you have on hand, and a list of what you need to buy. This not only saves you money, but it also prevents you from purchasing duplicates.

Check the offers

Before you go shopping, check the supermarket website to see what are the current promotional offers, discounts or deals. Don't skip this opportunity to save!

Buy in Bulk

Bulk purchasing can be a cost-effective way to stock up on cupboard staples. Stock up on store cupboard items that last, such as cans of lentils and chopped tomato tins or pasta and rice, when they are on sale.

Buy Frozen and dried Ingredients

Frozen and dried foods can often be less expensive than fresh foods and also have a much longer shelf life which can help reduce waste and save money in the long run.

Compare prices

To find the most affordable deal, compare the prices of items at various grocery stores.

Be Energy-Efficient

The cost of energy is skyrocketing. As a result, turning on the hop, or heating up the oven may cost you more than you are willing to spend. Save money by cooking with your Ninja Speedi Instead of using your oven. If you're wondering how much less expensive it is to run your ninja Speedi than a large oven. The difference is approximately 55% less overall your energy bill.

Foods to keep in your Cupboard, Fridge and Freezer:

Cooking is easier and faster when you already have the ingredients. A well stocked cupboard is the first step towards being able to prepare delicious food for your family while saving money. The rule here is to stock your cupboard just with ingredients that you are confident using and you enjoy eating.

Here`s a list of all important basics ...

1
Oil and vinegar

Olive oil, Vegetable oil and white vinegar.

2
Dairy

Eggs, Butter, Cheddar cheeses, Parmigiano Reggiano, Mozzarella, Milk, Double Cream.

3
Baking Essentials

Plain flour, cornflour, bicarbonate of soda, baking powder, vanilla essence, light soft brown sugar, caster sugar, icing sugar, runny honey, raisins or dried fruits.

4
Condiments

Dried herbs (make your own dried herbs by using the dehydration function in your Ninja Speedi), curry powder, ground cumin, smoked paprika, turmeric, English mustard, Worcestershire Sauce.

5
Tins and Packets

Tinned chopped tomatoes, tinned tuna, tinned salmon, tomato puree, pasta, long grain rice, lentils, pizza topper and tinned chickpeas.

6
Essential Vegetables

Potatoes (Maris Piper or King Edward), onion, garlic, celery, leeks and lemons.

7
Freezer Essentials

Frozen white fish fillets, frozen prawns, Frozen garden peas, cauliflower/broccoli florets, spinach, sausages, beef mince, boneless and skinless chicken thighs.

Note: **consider how frequently you will use these items and check expiration dates to ensure that nothing goes to waste.**

About the Recipes

In the next pages, you'll find a wide range of recipes that are both rich in flavour and affordable. We've included recipes that use inexpensive ingredients, these recipes are designed to be inexpensive, satisfying, and delicious.

About the cost per serving :

- The cost per serving is calculated based on an average of four UK supermarkets (Tesco, Asda, Sainsbury's, and Morrisons, etc).

- I have then used the average price across the four major supermarkets at the time of publishing.

- The cost per serving calculated by the amount used in the recipes, rather than the whole ingredient cost.

- The cost per serving does not include oil, herbs, seasoning, salt, or pepper, as we think you'll definitely have these.

BREAKFAST

Start your day right with these scrummy breakfast recipes.

Mushroom Tart

 Serving Size: 6  Cooking Time: 35 Minutes  Cost Per Serving: 53p

INGREDIENTS

Pastry :

- 230g plain flour
- 120g cold butter, cut into small cubes
- Cold water, as needed
- ½ tsp salt

Filling:

- 20g butter
- 1 onion, thinly sliced
- 2 garlic cloves, minced
- 500g mushroom, chopped
- 100ml double cream
- 5 large eggs
- 100g grated cheddar cheese
- Salt and pepper to taste

METHOD

1. In a bowl, add flour, butter, salt and rub with hands until it's like breadcrumbs. Add the water (2 tablespoons at a time), mix then bring together in a ball.

2. On a floured surface, roll out the pastry into ½-cm thick. Press the pastry into 20-cm tart tin. Cut out the excess pastry. Refrigerate.

3. Flip the SmartSwitch to AIR FRY/HOB. Select SEAR/SAUTÉ and set to 4 . Press START/STOP to begin cooking. Add the butter, add mushroom, garlic, and onion. Cook until all moisture absorbed. Press START/STOP to stop cooking. Transfer to a bowl.

4. Add eggs, cheese, salt, pepper and double cream to the mushroom mixture into the bowl. Whisk until combined.

5. Push in the legs on the Cook & Crisp tray, then place the tray in the bottom position in the pot. Place tart tin on the tray. Carefully fill with egg/mushroom mixture.

6. Close the lid and flip the SmartSwitch to AIR FRY/HOB, then use the centre arrows to select BAKE/ROAST. Set temperature to 175˚ C and set time to 30 minutes. Select START/STOP to begin cooking.
   When cooking is complete, remove from the unit and let it set for 10 minutes before serving.

11

Cheese and Onion Quiche

 *Serving Size:* 6    *Cooking Time:* 35 Minutes   £ *Cost Per Serving:* 50p

INGREDIENTS

Pastry :

- 230g plain flour
- 120g cold butter, cut into small cubes
- Cold water, as needed
- ½ tsp salt

Filling:

- 30g butter
- 1 large onion, thinly sliced
- 4 large eggs
- 100g grated cheddar cheese
- 3 tbsp chopped parsley
- 120ml milk
- 120ml double cream
- ½ tsp smoked paprika
- Salt & pepper to taste

METHOD

1. In a bowl, add flour, butter, salt and rub with hands until it's like breadcrumbs. Add the water (2 tablespoons at a time), mix then bring together in a ball.

2. Flip the SmartSwitch to AIR FRY/HOB. Select SEAR/SAUTÉ and set to 4 . Press START/STOP to begin cooking. Add add butter, onion and cook until soft. Transfer to a bowl and set aside until cooled slightly. Press START/STOP to stop cooking.

3. Grease 20-cm tart tin. On a floured surface, roll the pastry to ½-cm thick and line the tart tin with rolled pastry and line with baking paper, then fill with baking beans.

4. Rinse the inner pot. Place back pot into the Ninja Speedi. Push in the legs on the Cook & Crisp tray, then place the tray in the bottom position in the pot. Place tart tin on the tray.

5. Close the lid and flip the SmartSwitch to AIR FRY/HOB, then use the centre arrows to select BAKE/ROAST. Set temperature to 180˚ C and set time to 35 minutes. Select START/STOP to begin cooking.
   In a bowl, add eggs, onion mixture, milk, cheddar cheese, parsley, paprika, milk, cream, salt and pepper. Whisk until combined.

6. When time reaches 10 minutes, open the lid , carefully remove the baking beans and the baking paper. Pour in the egg mixture until it is two-thirds full. Do not overfill. Close lid to continue cooking.
   When cooking complete, open lid and remove the quiche . Serve hot or cold.

12

English Muffins

 *Serving Size: 8 English Muffins*

  *Cooking Time: 13 Minutes*

£ *Cost Per Serving: 20p*

INGREDIENTS

- 360g plain flour
- ¼ tsp dried yeast
- 1 tsp caster sugar
- Pinch of salt
- 140ml milk, lukewarm
- 120ml water, lukewarm
- 1 tbsp melted butter

METHOD

1. In a large bowl, add the flour, salt, sugar, yeast and mix until all combined. Add, the milk, water, melted butter and mix until a dough is formed.

2. Transfer the dough into a floured surface and knead for 5 minutes until smooth. Grease the bowl and place back the dough into the bowl. Cover with cling film and let it rise in a warm place for 30 minutes.

3. On a floured surface roll the dough into 2-cm in thickness. Use a biscuit cutter or a drinking glass to cut circles out of the dough.

4. Line the Cook & Crisp tray with baking paper or tin foil. Place the English muffins 1.5-cm apart on the lined tray. Cover and let rise for 35 minutes.

5. Add 250ml water to pot. Push in the legs on the Cook & Crisp tray, then place the tray in the bottom position in the pot.

6. Close the lid and flip the SmartSwitch to RAPID COOKER. Select STEAM BAKE, set temperature to 160° C and set time to 13 minutes. Select START/STOP to begin cooking.

7. When cooking is complete, remove the muffins from the ninja speedi, and let them cool on a wire rack.

13

Cheesy Eggy Toast

 *Serving Size: 4*    *Cooking Time: 15 Minutes*   £ *Cost Per Serving: 70p*

INGREDIENTS

- 4 medium eggs
- 6 tbsp milk
- 60g grated cheddar, finely grated
- 4 slices thick white bread
- 2 tbsp melted butter

METHOD

1. In a shallow dish, add eggs and whisk. Add the milk, cheddar and whisk until combined.

2. Add bread slices in the dish one slice at a time in the egg mixture, allowing it to soak for a few seconds.

3. Line the Cook & Crisp tray with tin foil. Place the bread slices on the lined tray.

4. Push in the legs on the Cook & Crisp tray, then place the tray in the bottom position in the pot.

5. Close the lid and flip the SmartSwitch to AIR FRY/HOB, then use the centre arrows to select BAKE/ROAST. Set temperature to 170° C and set time to 15 minutes. Select START/STOP to begin cooking.

6. When time reaches 10 minutes, open the lid and flip the bread. Close lid to continue cooking. When cooking is complete, serve.

Baked Egg and Tomatoes

 Serving Size: 4   Cooking Time: 23 Minutes £ Cost Per Serving: 60p

INGREDIENTS

- 400g baby tomatoes, halved if large
- 2 large garlic cloves, minced
- 2 tbsp oil
- 4 large eggs
- Salt and pepper to taste

METHOD

1. Add the tomatoes in Multi-Purpose Tin or 20-cm dish. Sprinkle with oil and add the minced garlic, season with salt and pepper. Stir.

2. Push in the legs on the Cook & Crisp tray, then place the tray in the bottom position in the pot. Place the tin on the tray.

3. Close the lid and flip the SmartSwitch to AIR FRY/HOB, then use the centre arrows to select BAKE/ROAST. Set temperature to 170° C and set time to 15 minutes. Select START/STOP to begin cooking.

4. When cooking is complete, open lid. Make four wells in the tomato mixture. Crack one egg in each well, sprinkle with salt and pepper.

5. Close the lid and flip the SmartSwitch to AIR FRY/HOB, then use the centre arrows to select BAKE/ROAST. Set temperature to 190° C and set time to 8 minutes. Select START/STOP to begin cooking.

6. When cooking is complete, remove from unit and serve with bread.

15

Cinnamon and Walnuts Porridge

 **Serving Size:** 4

 **Cooking Time:** 30 Minutes

£ **Cost Per Serving:** 42p

INGREDIENTS

- 150g porridge oats
- 2 tsp runny honey
- 1 tsp ground cinnamon
- 75g walnuts, chopped
- 600ml milk

METHOD

1. Add the porridge, milk, cinnamon and walnuts into the Ninja Speedi cooking pot. Stir.

2. Close the lid and flip the SmartSwitch to AIR FRY/HOB, then use the centre arrows to select BAKE/ROAST. Set temperature to 150° C and set time to 30 minutes. Select START/STOP to begin cooking.

3. When cooking is complete, open the lid, add the honey and stir, and serve topped with a sprinkle of cinnamon and chopped walnuts.

Tattie Scones

 Serving Size: 6-8    Cooking Time: 20 Minutes   £ Cost Per Serving: 30p

INGREDIENTS

- 500g Maris Piper, or King Edward potatoes, peeled, cooked, and mashed
- 2 tbsp melted butter
- Pinch of salt
- 120g plain flour
- 1 tsp baking powder
- Milk as needed

METHOD

1. In a large bowl, add the flour, salt, mashed potatoes, baking powder, melted butter. Mix until combined. Add the milk gradually until it form a dough. Continue to knead for 3 minutes until smooth. Divide into two equal portion.

2. On a floured surface roll each portion into ½-cm in thickness circle. Cut into wedges.

3. Line the Cook & Crisp tray with baking paper or tin foil. Place the scones on the lined tray.

4. Push in the legs on the Cook & Crisp tray, then place the tray in the bottom position in the pot.

5. Close the lid and flip the SmartSwitch to AIR FRY/HOB, then use the centre arrows to select BAKE/ROAST. Set temperature to 170° C and set time to 20 minutes. Select START/STOP to begin cooking.

6. When cooking is complete, remove the scones from the ninja speedi, and serve warm.

Cheesy Egg Bake

 *Serving Size: 2*    *Cooking Time: 12 Minutes*   £ *Cost Per Serving: 50p*

INGREDIENTS

- 2 medium tomatoes, chopped
- 4 large eggs
- 30g grated Parmigiano Reggiano
- 1 tbsp chopped fresh flat leaf parsley
- Salt and pepper to taste

METHOD

1. Grease two ramekins (8.5-cm) diameter. Arrange the tomato pieces in the bottom of the ramekins.

2. Crack two eggs in each ramekin, sprinkle with grated Parmigiano, salt and pepper. Stir gently.

3. Pour 200ml water into the pot. Push in the legs on the Cook & Crisp tray, then place the tray in the bottom position in the pot. Add ramekins on the tray.

4. Close the lid and flip the SmartSwitch to RAPID COOKER. Select STEAM BAKE, set temperature to 170° C and set time to 12 minutes. Select START/STOP to begin cooking.

5. When cooking is complete, remove the ramekins from the tray. Serve topped with parsley.

Courgette and Egg Bites

 *Serving Size:* 4    *Cooking Time:* 18 Minutes    *Cost Per Serving:* 50p

INGREDIENTS

- 2 medium courgettes, grated
- 6 large eggs
- 120ml milk
- 60g grated cheddar cheese
- 2 tbsp chopped fresh flat leaf parsley
- Salt and pepper to taste

METHOD

1. In a large bowl, add the eggs and milk and whisk until combined. Add the grated courgettes, cheddar , parsley, salt, and pepper. Mix until combined.

2. Grease 12 individual silicone muffin tins.

3. Push in the legs on the Cook & Crisp tray, then place tray in the bottom position in the pot. Place the muffin tins on top of the tray. Carefully pour the egg/courgette mixture evenly into the muffin tins about 3/4 way full.

4. Close the lid and flip the SmartSwitch to AIR FRY/HOB, then use the centre arrows to select BAKE/ROAST. Set temperature to 175° C and set time to 18 minutes until set and the edged are golden brown. Select START/STOP to begin cooking.

5. When cooking is complete, open lid and let it cool for a few minutes. Serve.

Cheese and Mushrooms Omelette

 *Serving Size:* 4    *Cooking Time:* 13 Minutes   £ *Cost Per Serving:* 75p

INGREDIENTS

- 8 large eggs
- 225g mushrooms, sliced
- 1 tbsp oil
- 2 tbsp butter
- 120ml milk
- 60g grated cheddar cheese
- Salt and pepper to taste

METHOD

1. In a large bowl, add the eggs, cheese, salt, pepper, milk and whisk until combined.

2. Flip the SmartSwitch to AIR FRY/HOB. Select SEAR/SAUTÉ and set to 4 . Press START/STOP to begin cooking. Add the butter, then add mushrooms. Cook for 8 minutes until soft and most of the liquid evaporated. Press START/STOP to stop cooking. Transfer mushroom into the egg mixture bowl and stir.

3. Grease Multi-Purpose Tin or 20cm cake tin with oil, pour the egg/mushroom mixture into the tin.

4. Add 500ml water to pot. Push in the legs on the Cook & Crisp tray, then place tray in the bottom position in the pot. Place the tin on top of the tray.

5. Close the lid and flip the SmartSwitch to RAPID COOKER. Select STEAM BAKE and set time to 13 minutes and temperature to 160° C. Select START/STOP to begin cooking

6. When cooking is complete, open lid and let it cool for a few minutes.
   Cut the omelette into quarters and serve hot.

20

Starters and Sides

Start your dinner with delicious sides and starters.

Stuffed Hasselback Potatoes

 *Serving Size:* 4    *Cooking Time:* 46 Minutes   £ *Cost Per Serving:* 80p

INGREDIENTS

- 4 large Maris Piper potatoes
- 1 tbsp oil
- 40g unsalted butter, room temperature
- 100g pepperoni, chopped
- 150g grated cheddar

METHOD

1. Place one of the potatoes on a chopping board in between the handles of 2 wooden spoons. Using a sharp knife cut the potato crosswise into ½-cm thick slices (Do not cut all the way through). Repeat with the remaining potatoes.

2. Rub each potato with oil and stuff in between the slices with softened butter.

3. Pour 250ml water into the pot. Push in the legs on the Cook & Crisp tray, then place the tray in the bottom position in the pot. Add potatoes on the tray.

4. Close the lid and flip the SmartSwitch to RAPID COOKER. Select STEAM AIR FRY, set temperature to 200° C and set time to 40 minutes. Select START/STOP to begin cooking.

5. When cooking is complete, open the lid and stuff the sliced slots with cheddar and pepperoni.

6. Close the lid and flip the SmartSwitch to RAPID COOKER. Select STEAM AIR FRY, set temperature to 200° C and set time to 6 minutes until cheese is melted. Select START/STOP to begin cooking. Serve.

Courgette and Cheddar Fritters

 *Serving Size:* 4    *Cooking Time:* 19 Minutes   £ *Cost Per Serving:* 80p

INGREDIENTS

- 300g grated courgette
- 300g potatoes, peeled and grated
- 3 large eggs
- 1 tsp onion powder
- 1 tsp garlic powder
- 40g plain flour
- 30g breadcrumbs
- 1 tsp bicarbonate of soda
- 100g grated mature cheddar cheese
- Salt and pepper to taste

METHOD

1. Squeeze the liquid out of the grated courgette and potatoes as much as possible.

2. Transfer the courgette and potatoes to a bowl, add all remaining ingredients and stir until all combined. Divide into 8 portions. Shape into burger shapes.

3. Push in the legs on the Cook & Crisp tray, then place the tray in the bottom position in the pot, line with baking paper. Place fritters on the lined tray.

4. Close the lid and flip the SmartSwitch to AIR FRY/HOB, then use the centre arrows to select AIR FRY. Set temperature to 175° C and set time to 19 minutes. Select START/STOP to begin cooking.

5. When the time reaches 10 minutes, open lid, flip the fritter and close lid to continue cooking.

6. When cooking is complete, open lid and serve warm.

Roasted Potatoes with Rosemary and Garlic

 *Serving Size: 4*    *Cooking Time: 25 Minutes*   £ *Cost Per Serving: 30p*

INGREDIENTS

- 1 kg baby potatoes, halved if large
- 6 garlic cloves, whole
- 1 tbsp fresh thyme leaves, chopped
- 1 tbsp fresh rosemary leaves, chopped
- 3 tbsp oil or melted duck/goose fat
- Salt and pepper to taste

METHOD

1. In a large bowl, add all ingredients and mix until all potatoes coated with seasoning and oil.

2. Pour 300ml water into the pot. Push in the legs on the Cook & Crisp tray, then place the tray in the bottom position in the pot. Add potatoes on the tray.

3. Close the lid and flip the SmartSwitch to RAPID COOKER. Select STEAM AIR FRY, set temperature to 210˚ C and set time to 25 minutes. Select START/STOP to begin cooking.

4. When the time reaches 10 minutes, open lid, flip the potatoes and close lid to continue cooking.

5. When cooking is complete, use tongs to remove the potatoes from the tray. Serve.

Leek and Potato Soup

 *Serving Size: 6*  *Cooking Time: 4 hours* £ *Cost Per Serving: 27p*

INGREDIENTS

- 30g butter
- 1 tbsp oil
- 3 leeks, chopped
- 1 onion, chopped
- 1.5 L chicken stock
- 2 large potatoes, peeled and cubed
- Salt and pepper to taste
- 100ml double cream

METHOD

1. Flip the SmartSwitch to AIR FRY/HOB. Select SEAR/SAUTÉ and set to 3 . Press START/STOP to begin cooking. Add the butter and oil , then add leeks and onion. Cook for 6 minutes. Press START/STOP to stop cooking.

2. Add the chicken stock, potatoes, salt, pepper and stir.

3. Close the lid, flip the SmartSwitch to AIR FRY/HOB, then use the centre arrows select SLOW COOK, set temperature to HIGH and time to 4 hours (or LOW for 6 hours). Select START/STOP to begin cooking.

4. When cooking is complete, blend with a hand or regular blender until smooth. Add the double cream, adjust seasoning, stir and serve.

Celeriac Soup

 *Serving Size:* 4    *Cooking Time:* 15 Minutes   £ *Cost Per Serving:* 50p

INGREDIENTS

- 1 tbsp oil
- 1 kg celeriac, peeled and chopped into small pieces
- 250g potatoes, peeled and chopped into small pieces
- 4 garlic cloves, minced
- 2 celery stalks, sliced
- 1 medium onion, chopped

- 1 bay leaf
- 1 tsp dried thyme
- 1.5 litre vegetable stock
- 150ml double cream
- Salt and pepper to taste

METHOD

1. Flip the SmartSwitch to AIR FRY/HOB. Select SEAR/SAUTÉ and set to "4". Press START/STOP to begin cooking. Add oil to the pot. Add the onion and celery. Cook until soft. Add the garlic and cook for a minute. Select START/STOP to stop cooking.

2. Add all remaining ingredients into the cooking pot (except cream), stir.

3. Close the lid and flip the SmartSwitch to RAPID COOKER. Select SPEEDI MEALS and set the temperature to 180° C and time to 15 minutes. Select START/STOP to begin cooking.

4. When cooking is complete, open lid, stir and then blind with a blender until smooth.

5. Add the double cream and adjust seasoning. Transfer into bowls and serve.

Cotswold Dumplings

 *Serving Size:* 4    *Cooking Time:* 10 Minutes   £ *Cost Per Serving:* 25p

INGREDIENTS

- 50g butter, softened
- 110g grated cheddar cheese
- 3 eggs, beaten
- 4 spring onions, finely chopped
- 4 tsp milk
- 170g fresh breadcrumbs
- 20g dried breadcrumbs
- Salt and pepper to taste

METHOD

1. In bowl, add butter, spring onion, cheese and mix until combined. Add milk, eggs, salt, pepper, fresh breadcrumbs, Mix until combined and shape into 16 balls, then coat with the dried breadcrumbs, brush with oil.

2. Push in the legs on the Cook & Crisp tray, then place tray in the bottom position in the pot. Add the dumplings on the tray.

3. Close the lid and flip the SmartSwitch to AIR FRY/HOB, then use the centre arrows to select BAKE/ROAST. Set temperature to 175° C and set time to 10 minutes until golden. Select START/STOP to begin cooking.

4. When time reaches 4 minutes, open lid and flip the dumpling. Close lid to continue cooking.

5. When the cooking is complete, use silicone coated tongs to remove the dumplings to a serving dish and serve.

Irish Pan Haggerty

 Serving Size: 4    Cooking Time: 55 Minutes   £ Cost Per Serving: 50p

INGREDIENTS

- 700g Maris Piper or King Edward potatoes, peeled and thinly sliced
- 1 large onion, finely chopped
- 2 tbsp oil
- 1 tsp ground nutmeg
- 150g grated cheddar cheese
- 240ml chicken stock
- Salt and pepper to taste

METHOD

1. Flip the SmartSwitch to AIR FRY/HOB. Select SEAR/SAUTÉ and set to 3. Press START/STOP to begin. Add oil, onion, cook until soft. Select START/STOP to stop cooking.

2. Grease 20-cm deep pie dish. Layer ⅓ of potatoes, then ⅓ of onion and a ⅓ of the cheddar and finally sprinkle with the nutmeg, salt and pepper. Repeat layering until all the ingredients are used. Pour in the chicken stock. Cover with tin foil.

3. Push in the legs on the Cook & Crisp tray, then place the tray in the bottom position in the pot. Add the dish on the tray.

4. Close the lid and flip the SmartSwitch to AIR FRY/HOB, then use the centre arrows to select BAKE/ROAST. Set temperature to 170˚ C and set time to 50 minutes until tender. Select START/STOP to begin cooking.

5. When time reaches 40 minutes, open lid, remove foil. Close lid to continue cooking.

Mains

Main dish ideas for the family that are both excellent and cheap.

Scotch Eggs

 *Serving Size:* 4    *Cooking Time:* 25 Minutes   £ *Cost Per Serving:* 42p

INGREDIENTS

- 4 eggs, boiled for 5 minutes and peeled
- 400g sausage meat
- 1 tsp onion powder
- 1 tsp dried thyme
- 2 tsp English mustard
- 100g white breadcrumbs
- 60g plain flour
- 2 eggs
- Salt and Pepper to taste

METHOD

1. In a bowl, add sausage meat, onion powder, thyme , mustard, salt and pepper. Mix until combined and divide into four equal portions.

2. In a bowl, add flour. In another bowl add the 2 eggs and whisk. In a third bowl, add the breadcrumbs.

3. Roll a boiled egg in flour, wrap each boiled egg with the sausage meat mixture.

4. Roll each wrapped eggs in flour, then in egg and finally coat with breadcrumbs. Brush with oil.

5. Push in the legs on the Cook & Crisp tray, then place tray in the bottom position in the pot. Add the scotch eggs on the tray.

6. Close the lid and flip the SmartSwitch to AIR FRY/HOB, then use the centre arrows to select BAKE/ROAST. Set temperature to 190° C and set time to 25 minutes until golden. Select START/STOP to begin cooking.

5. When time reaches 12 minutes, open lid and flip the scotch eggs. Close lid to continue cooking. When cooking is complete, open lid and remove the scotch eggs. Serve with HP sauce.

Minced Beef and Rice Casserole

 *Serving Size: 4*  *Cooking Time: 15 Minutes* £ *Cost Per Serving: £1*

INGREDIENTS

- 2 tbsp oil
- 400g beef mince
- 1 large onion, finely chopped
- 2 cloves garlic, minced
- 1 celery stalk, finely chopped
- 1 tsp smoked paprika
- 450g uncooked long grain rice, rinsed until water runs clear
- 1 litre vegetable or chicken stock
- 2 tbsp Worcestershire sauce
- Salt and pepper to taste
- Handful chopped flat leaf parsley

METHOD

1. Flip the SmartSwitch to AIR FRY/HOB. Select SEAR/SAUTÉ and set to 4 . Press START/STOP to begin cooking. Add the oil to the pot. Add the onion. Cook until soft. Add mince and cook until brown for about 5 minutes. Select START/STOP to stop cooking.

2. Add all remaining ingredients into the pot. Stir.

3. Close the lid and flip the SmartSwitch to RAPID COOKER. Select STEAM BAKE and set the temperature to 200° C and time to 15 minutes. Select START/STOP to begin cooking.

4. When cooking is complete, open lid, stir the rice. Serve topped with parsley.

31

Beef Curry

 Serving Size: 4    Cooking Time: 5 hours   £ Cost Per Serving: £1.50

INGREDIENTS

- 2 tbsp oil
- 400g stewing beef, cut into bite size pieces
- 2 large onions, chopped
- 4 garlic cloves, minced
- 4 Maris Piper potatoes, cut into 2-cm cubes
- 1 large carrot, sliced
- ½ tsp ginger powder
- 1 tsp ground cumin
- 2 tbsp curry powder
- 3 tbsp tomato puree
- 1 (400g) tin chopped tomatoes
- 600ml beef stock

METHOD

1. Flip the SmartSwitch to AIR FRY/HOB. Select SEAR/SAUTÉ and set to 4 . Press START/STOP to begin cooking. Add oil , add the beef and brown on all sides. Transfer to a plate and set aside.

2. Add the onion to the cooking pot, cook until soft. Add the garlic and all the spices and cook for a minute. Press START/STOP to stop cooking. Add all remaining ingredients and stir.

3. Close the lid, flip the SmartSwitch to AIR FRY/HOB, then use the centre arrows select SLOW COOK, set temperature to HIGH and time to 5 hours (or LOW for 8 hours). Select START/STOP to begin cooking.

4. When cooking is complete, stir and serve with rice.

Bangers and Colcannon

 Serving Size: 4-6    Cooking Time: 15 Minutes   £ Cost Per Serving: £1

INGREDIENTS

Tray
- 8 Sausages (bangers)
- 2 tbsp oil

Bottom of the pot:
- 1 kg potatoes, peeled and cut into 2-cm cubes
- 500g cabbage, cut into 1-cm pieces
- 4 spring onions, chopped

- 200ml water
- 60g unsalted butter
- 50ml milk
- 60ml double cream
- Salt and pepper to taste

METHOD

1. Place the potatoes, water and salt in the Ninja Speedi Pot, stir.

2. Pull out the legs on the Cook & Crisp tray, then place tray in the top position in the pot, above the potatoes. Place the sausages on top of the tray. Brush with oil.

3. Close the lid and flip the SmartSwitch to RAPID COOKER. Select SPEEDI MEALS and set the temperature to 185° C and time to 12 minutes. Select START/STOP to begin cooking.

4. When cooking is complete, open lid and transfer the sausages to a plate and loosely cover with tin foil. Then use silicone-tipped tongs to grab the centre handle and remove the tray from the unit.

5. Place the cabbage in to the pot on top of the potatoes. Close the lid, Select SPEEDI MEALS and set the temperature to 190° C and time to 3 minutes, then select START/STOP to begin cooking.

6. When cooking is complete, open lid, add the milk, double cream, butter, spring onion, salt and pepper. Mash with a potato masher.
Serve the colcannon with sausages.

33

Beef and Mushroom Casserole

 **Serving Size:** 4

 **Cooking Time:** 30 Minutes

 **Cost Per Serving:** £1.10

INGREDIENTS

- 500g stewing beef or beef stir fry strips, diced or sliced
- 225 g mushrooms, sliced
- 1 large onion, chopped
- 3 garlic cloves, minced
- 2 tbsp oil, divided
- 2 tbsp plain flour
- 1 litre beef stock

- 1 tbsp Worcestershire sauce
- 1 tsp dried thyme
- Salt and pepper, to taste

METHOD

1. Flip the SmartSwitch to AIR FRY/HOB. Select SEAR/SAUTÉ and set to HI 5. Press START/STOP to begin. Add 1 tbsp oil to cooking pot. Add the beef and cook until browned on all sides. Transfer to a plate and set aside.

2. Add 1 tbsp oil to the cooking pot, add the onion, and garlic. Cook for 5 minutes. Add the flour and stir until combined. Select START/STOP to end cooking. Place back the beef along with all remaining ingredients (except mushroom) and stir.

3. Close the lid and flip the SmartSwitch to RAPID COOKER. Select STEAM BAKE and set the temperature to 170° C and time to 20 minutes. Select START/STOP to begin cooking.

4. When cooking is complete, open lid and add the mushroom, stir (add 500ml water if the stew is too thick).

5. Close the lid and flip the SmartSwitch to RAPID COOKER. Select STEAM BAKE and set the temperature to 170° C and time to 10 minutes. Select START/STOP to begin cooking.

6. When cooking is complete, open lid, stir. Serve with rice or bread.

Lamb and Vegetables Skewers

 *Serving Size:* 4    *Cooking Time:* 20 Minutes   £ *Cost Per Serving:* £1.20

INGREDIENTS

- 450 g lamb leg steaks, cut into 2 ½-cm cubes
- 1 red bell pepper, cut into 2 ½-cm pieces
- 1 green bell pepper, cut into 2 ½-cm pieces
- 1 large onion, cut into 2 ½-cm pieces
- 150g butternut squash, cut into 2 ½-cm cubes
- 8 small tomatoes
- 2 tbsp oil
- 1 tsp garlic powder
- 1 tsp smoked paprika
- Salt and pepper to taste
- 8-10 skewers, soaked in water for 30 minutes

METHOD

1. In a bowl, mix together oil, garlic powder, smoked paprika, salt, and pepper. Add the vegetables and beef and stir until all coated with seasoning.

2. Thread the beef, bell peppers, butternut squash, onion and tomato onto the skewers, alternating between the beef and vegetables.

3. Pull out the legs on the Cook & Crisp tray, then place tray in the top position in the pot. Place the skewers on top of the tray.

4. Close the lid and flip the SmartSwitch to AIR FRY/HOB, then use the centre arrows to select GRILL. Set temperature to 200° C and set time to 10 minutes. Select START/STOP to begin cooking.

5. When time reaches 5 minutes, open lid and flip the skewers. Close lid to continue cooking.

6. When cooking is complete, Serve the skewers with rice or salad.

Sausage with Onions and Peppers

 Serving Size: 4

 Cooking Time: 15 Minutes

£ Cost Per Serving: £1

INGREDIENTS

- Tray:
- 450g English sausage
- 2 tbsp oil

Bottom of the pot:

- 2 red bell peppers, sliced
- 2 large onions, sliced
- ½ tsp dried oregano
- 3 garlic cloves, minced
- 1 (400g) tin chopped tomatoes
- 2 tbsp tomato puree
- 200ml water
- Salt and pepper to taste

METHOD

1. Place all the pot ingredients in the Ninja Speedi Pot, stir.

2. Pull out the legs on the Cook & Crisp tray, then place tray in the top position in the pot. Place the sausages on top of the tray. Brush with oil.

3. Close the lid and flip the SmartSwitch to RAPID COOKER. Select SPEEDI MEALS and set the temperature to 190° C and time to 15 minutes. Select START/STOP to begin cooking.

4. When time reaches 5 minutes, open lid and flip the sausages. Close lid to continue cooking.

5. When cooking is complete, use tongs to remove the sausages from the tray and transfer to a plate. Remove the tray.

6. Place back the sausages into the onion and pepper mixture. Stir and serve with bread.

Minced Beef and Potato Casserole

 *Serving Size: 6*    *Cooking Time: 30 Minutes*    *Cost Per Serving: £ 1.25*

INGREDIENTS

- 1 tsp oil
- 2 garlic cloves, minced
- 500g King Edward Potatoes, peeled, thinly sliced
- 400g beef mince
- 1 large onion, finely chopped
- 1 carrot, finely chopped

- 1 large courgette, sliced
- 240ml beef stock
- 1 (400g) tin chopped tomatoes
- 200g frozen spinach, defrosted and drained
- 120g grated mature cheddar cheese
- 120ml double cream
- Salt and pepper to taste

METHOD

1. Flip the SmartSwitch to AIR FRY/HOB. Select SEAR/SAUTÉ and set to "3". Press START/STOP to begin cooking. Add oil, mince and cook until browned. Add onion and garlic and cook for 3 minutes. Add courgette, tomatoes and stock. Simmer for 4 minutes. Add the defrosted spinach, salt, pepper and stir. Select START/STOP to stop cooking.

2. Grease 20-cm deep pie dish, place ½ of the mince mixture into the dish. Spread ½ of the sliced potato over the mince. Repeat layering. Pour the cream on top and sprinkle with cheddar.

3. Rinse the cooking pot and place back in the Ninja Speedi. Push in the legs on the Cook & Crisp tray, then place tray in the bottom position in the pot. Place the pie dish on top of the tray.

4. Close the lid and flip the SmartSwitch to AIR FRY/HOB, then use the centre arrows to select BAKE/ROAST. Set temperature to 170˚ C and time to 40 minutes. Select START/STOP to begin cooking.

5. When cooking is complete, remove from unit and serve.

This Minced Beef and Potato Casserole has everything you need for a tasty meal. Creamy potatoes topped with seasoned minced beef makes the perfect comfort dinner that the whole family will enjoy.

Minced Beef Hotpot

 Serving Size: 4

 Cooking Time: 50 Minutes

£ Cost Per Serving: 90p

INGREDIENTS

- 1 tbsp oil
- 400g beef mince
- 1 large onion, finely chopped
- 3 medium carrots, peeled and chopped
- 250g parsnips, peeled and chopped
- 150g frozen garden peas
- 2 tbsp plain flour
- 500ml beef stock
- 1 tsp Worcestershire Sauce

- 500g potatoes, thinly sliced
- Salt and pepper to taste

METHOD

1. Flip the SmartSwitch to AIR FRY/HOB. Select SEAR/SAUTÉ and set to "4". Press START/STOP to begin cooking. Add 1 tbsp oil to the pot. Add the onion. Cook until soft. Add the minced beef and cook until browned. Add the flour and stir until combined.

2. Add all remaining ingredients to the cooking pot (except potatoes) and stir until combined. Simmer for 7 minutes, then Select START/STOP to stop cooking.

3. Transfer the mince mixture into deep pie dish. Layer the potato slices over the top. Cover with tin foil.

4. Rinse the inner pot and place back in the Ninja Speedi. Push in the legs on the Cook & Crisp tray, then place tray in the bottom position in the pot. Place the pie dish on top of the tray.

5. Close the lid and flip the SmartSwitch to AIR FRY/HOB, then use the centre arrows to select BAKE/ROAST. Set temperature to 180° C and set time to 50 minutes. Select START/STOP to begin cooking.

6. When time reaches 40 minutes, open lid and remove the tin foil and brush with oil. Close lid to continue cooking.
   When cooking is complete, open lid, remove from the unit. Serve with bread.

39

Beef Mince Curry

 **Serving Size:** 4     **Cooking Time:** 5 Minutes   £ **Cost Per Serving:** £1

INGREDIENTS

- 500g beef mince
- 1 tbsp oil
- 1 onion, chopped
- 2 garlic cloves, minced
- 1 celery stalk, sliced
- 1 tsp ginger powder
- 1 tsp cumin seeds
- 1 tsp ground coriander
- 1 tsp turmeric
- 1 tsp chilli powder
- 2 tbsp tomato puree
- 1 (400g) tin chopped tomatoes
- 200ml water
- 1 red pepper, chopped
- 1 green pepper, chopped
- Salt and pepper to taste

METHOD

1. Flip the SmartSwitch to AIR FRY/HOB. Select SEAR/SAUTÉ and set to 4. Press START/STOP to begin. Add oil to cooking pot. Add the onion and cook until softened. Add the mince and cook, breaking it up with a wooden spoon for 3 minutes.

2. Add the garlic and all the seasoning and cook for a minute. Select START/STOP to stop cooking. Add all remaining ingredients and stir.

3. Close the lid and flip the SmartSwitch to RAPID COOKER. Select STEAM BAKE and set the temperature to 190° C and time to 5 minutes. Select START/STOP to begin cooking.

4. When cooking is complete, open lid, transfer to serving plates, and serve with rice.

Beef Stew with Dumplings

 *Serving Size: 4*

  *Cooking Time: 4 Hours 20 mins*

£ *Cost Per Serving: £1.20*

INGREDIENTS

- 800g diced beef
- 2 tbsp plain flour
- 2 tbsp oil
- 1 large onion, finely chopped
- 4 garlic cloves , minced
- 2 large carrots, chopped
- 2 large potatoes, peeled and chopped
- 800ml beef stock
- 1 (400g) tin chopped tomatoes
- 2 bay leaves
- 1 tsp dried thyme
- Salt and pepper to taste

For the Dumplings:
- 130g self-raising flour
- 120g cold butter, cut into cubes
- Cold milk as needed
- Salt to taste

METHOD

1. Flip the SmartSwitch to AIR FRY/HOB. Select SEAR/SAUTÉ and set to 4. Press START/STOP to begin. Add oil to cooking pot. Add the the diced beef and cook until browned on all sides. Remove the beef from the cooking pot and set aside.

2. Add the onion, garlic, carrots and potatoes to the cooking pot. Cook for 6 minutes. Add the flour and stir until combined. Gradually add the beef stock while stirring. Add the bay leaves, chopped tomatoes, thyme, salt, and pepper. Stir and add back the beef to the pot. Select START/STOP to stop cooking.

3. Close the lid, select SLOW COOK, set temperature to HIGH and time to 4 hours. Select START/STOP to begin cooking.

4. In a bowl, add flour, salt and butter. Rub butter into the flour until resembles breadcrumbs. Add milk gradually while mixing until the dough comes together. Roll into 6-8 small balls.

5. When cooking is complete, open lid, add the dumpling over the stew.

6. Close the lid and flip the SmartSwitch to AIR FRY/HOB, then use the centre arrows to select BAKE/ROAST. Set temperature to 170° C and set time to 20 minutes. Select START/STOP to begin cooking.
   When cooking is complete, Serve the stew topped with the dumpling.

41

Beef and Baked Beans Lasagne

 *Serving Size: 6*    *Cooking Time: 30 Minutes*   £ *Cost Per Serving: 90p*

INGREDIENTS

- 1 tbsp oil
- 1 onion, chopped
- 2 garlic cloves
- 250g beef mince
- 1 (400g) tin baked beans In tomato sauce
- 1 (400g) tin chopped tomatoes
- 100ml water
- Lasagne pasta
- 50g mozzarella cheese
- 50g grated Cheddar cheese
- Salt and pepper to taste

METHOD

1. Flip the SmartSwitch to AIR FRY/HOB. Select SEAR/SAUTÉ and set to 4 . Press START/STOP to begin cooking. Add the oil to the pot. Add the onion, and beef mince. Cook, stirring occasionally until browned through. Add the baked beans, water, garlic, chopped tomato, salt and pepper. Allow to simmer for 5 minutes. Select START/STOP to stop cooking.

2. In a baking tin that will fit in your Ninja Speedi, add a layer of beef and bean mixture and cover with a layer of pasta sheets, sprinkle with cheddar cheese. Repeat the layers of meat, pasta and cheddar until you have four layer. Finish by sprinkling the top with mozzarella cheese.

3. Rinse the inner pot and place back in the Ninja Speedi. Push in the legs on the Cook & Crisp tray, then place tray in the bottom position in the pot. Place the baking tin on top of the tray.

4. Close the lid and flip the SmartSwitch to AIR FRY/HOB, then use the centre arrows to select BAKE/ROAST. Set temperature to 170˚ C and set time to 30 minutes. Select START/STOP to begin cooking.

5. When cooking is complete, open lid, transfer to serving plates, and serve.

42

Minced Beef Stuffed Aubergine

 *Serving Size:* 4    *Cooking Time: 12 Minutes*   £ *Cost Per Serving: 90p*

INGREDIENTS

- 1 tbsp oil
- 4 medium aubergines
- 500g minced beef
- 1 onion, finely chopped
- 2 garlic cloves, minced
- ½ tsp dried basil
- ½ tsp dried oregano
- 1 (400g) tin chopped tomatoes
- Salt and pepper to taste

METHOD

1. Make a slit lengthwise in each aubergine and scoop out the flesh, leaving a shell about 2-cm thick. Chop the flesh into small pieces and set aside.

2. Flip the SmartSwitch to AIR FRY/HOB. Select SEAR/SAUTÉ and set to HI 5. Press START/STOP to begin. Add oil to the pot and add the onion. Cook for 3 minutes. Add the mince and brown for 5 minutes. Add the chopped aubergine flesh, chopped tomatoes, oregano, basil, salt, and pepper. Cook for 7 minutes. Select START/STOP to stop cooking.

3. Stuff the aubergine shells with the mince mixture. (freeze any leftover mince mixture in a freezer bag for up to 4 months, and use it on pasta)

4. Add 200ml water to the pot. Push in the legs on the Cook & Crisp tray, then place the tray in the bottom position in the pot. Place the aubergines on the tray.

5. Close the lid and flip the SmartSwitch to RAPID COOKER. Select STEAM BAKE and set the temperature to 190° C and time to 12 minutes. Select START/STOP to begin cooking.

6. When cooking is complete, open lid and Let cool for a few minutes before serving.

43

Haggis Burger

 **Serving Size:** 6  **Cooking Time:** 8 Minutes £ **Cost Per Serving:** 90p

INGREDIENTS

- 300g haggis, crumbled
- 500g beef mince
- 2 garlic cloves, minced
- 120g grated cheddar
- Salt and pepper to taste

METHOD

1. In a bowl add all ingredients and mix until combined. Divide mixture into 6 equal portions. and shape each portion into a patty.

2. Push in the legs on the Cook & Crisp tray, then place the tray in the bottom position in the pot. Place the burgers on the tray.

3. Close the lid and flip the SmartSwitch to AIR FRY/HOB. Select AIR FRY and set the temperature to 190˚ C and time to 8 minutes. Select START/STOP to begin cooking.

4. When time reaches 4 minutes, open lid and flip burgers. Close lid to continue cooking.

5. When cooking is complete, remove from unit. Serve with with your favourite toppings (lettuce, tomato, and sauces you like).

Pasta and Meatballs

 *Serving Size: 5*    *Cooking Time: 5 Minutes*   £ *Cost Per Serving: £1.28*

INGREDIENTS

Bottom of pot:

- 1 tsp oil
- 4 basil leaves
- 1 onion, chopped
- 2 garlic cloves, minced
- 2 (400g) tins chopped tomatoes
- 600ml water or stock
- 400g dried spaghetti, (split in half) or penne
- ½ tsp dried or fresh chopped basil
- ½ tsp Worcestershire sauce

Tray:

- 500g minced beef
- 20g white breadcrumbs
- ½ tsp Worcestershire sauce
- 1 tbsp dried oregano
- 1 egg
- 1 tbsp dried rosemary
- Salt and pepper to tast

METHOD

1. In a bowl, add all tray ingredients and mix until combined. With wet hands divide mixture into 24 meatballs. Brush with oil and set aside.

2. Flip the SmartSwitch to AIR FRY/HOB. Select SEAR/SAUTÉ and set to 4. Press START/STOP to begin. Add oil to the pot and add the garlic and onion. Cook for 3 minutes. Select START/STOP to stop cooking. Add the chopped tomato, stock, Worcestershire sauce, basil and pasta to the pot. Season with salt, pepper and stir.

3. Push in the legs on the Cook & Crisp tray, then place the tray in the bottom position in the pot. Place meatballs on the tray. Brush with oil.

4. Close the lid and flip the SmartSwitch to RAPID COOKER. Select STEAM AIR FRY and set the temperature to 180° C and time to 15 minutes. Select START/STOP to begin cooking.

5. When cooking is complete, transfer meatballs to a plate. Then use silicone-tipped tongs to grab the centre handle and remove the tray from the unit.

6. Place the meatballs back into the pasta, let sit for 5 minutes. Stir and serve.

45

Sausage Rigatoni

 *Serving Size:* 4    *Cooking Time:* 12 Minutes   £ *Cost Per Serving:* 93p

INGREDIENTS

Bottom of the pot:

- 1 tsp oil
- Hnadful fresh spinach
- 225g rigatoni or penne pasta
- 400g tin chopped tomatoes
- 500ml vegetable stock
- 1 tsp sugar
- 2 tsp Worcestershire sauce
- 3 tbsp tomato puree
- 3 garlic cloves, minced
- 1 small onion, finely chopped

- 1 tsp dried oregano
- Salt and pepper to taste
- 50g fresh spinach (optional)

Tray:

- 400g sausage

METHOD

1. Flip the SmartSwitch to AIR FRY/HOB. Select SEAR/SAUTÉ and set to 3 Press START/STOP to begin. Add oil to the pot and add the garlic and onion. Cook for 3 minutes. Select START/STOP to stop cooking. Add the chopped tomato, stock, Worcestershire sauce, oregano and pasta to the pot. Season with salt, pepper and stir.

2. Push in the legs on the Cook & Crisp tray, then place the tray in the bottom position in the pot. Place sausages on the tray. Brush with oil.

3. Close the lid and flip the SmartSwitch to RAPID COOKER. Select STEAM AIR FRY and set the temperature to 190° C and time to 12 minutes. Select START/STOP to begin cooking.

4. When cooking is complete, open lid and carefully remove the sausage. Chop the sausage into smaller pieces and place back into the pasta along with the spinach. Stir and serve.

46

Chicken Fajitas

 *Serving Size: 4*

 *Cooking Time: 15 Minutes*

£ *Cost Per Serving: £1.40*

INGREDIENTS

- Juice of one lemon, divided
- 2 tbsp oil
- 700g boneless, skinless chicken thighs or breasts, cut into strips
- 1 tsp garlic powder
- 1 tsp onion powder
- 1 tsp smoked paprika
- ½ tsp ground cumin
- 1 medium onion, sliced
- 1 of each (yellow, red and green bell peppers), sliced

To serve:
- 4 large flour tortillas

METHOD

1. In a large bowl, add all ingredients and mix until all chicken pieces coated with seasoning and oil.

2. Push in the legs on the Cook & Crisp tray, then place the tray in the bottom position in the pot. Add the chicken and bell pepper mixture on the tray.

3. Close the lid and flip the SmartSwitch to AIR FRY/HOB, then use the centre arrows to select BAKE/ROAST. Set temperature to 200° C and set time to 15 minutes. Select START/STOP to begin cooking.

4. When the time reaches 8 minutes, open lid, mix the chicken /pepper mixture and close lid to continue cooking.

    When cooking is complete, remove from unit. Serve with tortillas.

Coronation Chicken

 *Serving Size:* **4**    *Cooking Time:* **15 Minutes**   £ *Cost Per Serving:* **£1.30**

INGREDIENTS

- 1 tbsp oil
- 1 small onion, finely chopped
- 1 bay leaf
- 3 small apricots, finely chopped
- 2 tsp curry powder
- 1 tsp tomato puree
- 100 ml chicken stock
- 200g mayonnaise
- 120g double cream
- Salt and pepper to taste

METHOD

1. Season the chicken pieces with salt and pepper. Brush with oil.

2. Push in the legs on the Cook & Crisp tray, then place the tray in the bottom position in the pot. Add the chicken on the tray.

3. Close the lid and flip the SmartSwitch to AIR FRY/HOB, then use the centre arrows to select BAKE/ROAST. Set temperature to 190° C and set time to 9 minutes. Select START/STOP to begin cooking.

4. When cooking is complete, remove the chicken from unit into a plate and set aside. Then use silicone-tipped tongs to grab the centre handle and remove the tray from the unit.

5. Flip the SmartSwitch to AIR FRY/HOB. Select SEAR/SAUTÉ and set to 4. Press START/STOP to begin. Add oil to the pot. Cook until soft. Add the 1 bay leaf, curry powder, stock, tomato puree, water. Stir and simmer for 3 minutes. Select START/STOP to stop cooking. Let cool completely.

6. Strain the sauce into a bowl. Add the double cream, mayonnaise, and apricots. Mix until combined. Add the chicken pieces into the mixture and mix until the chicken coated with the sauce. Serve with a salad or in sandwiches.

48

Chicken and Mushroom Pie

 *Serving Size: 6-8*    *Cooking Time: 40 Minutes*   £ *Cost Per Serving: £1.50*

INGREDIENTS

Pastry:

- 400g plain flour
- 1 tsp salt
- 200g unsalted butter, cold and cut into small cubes
- Cold water as needed

Pie filling:

- 500g boneless, skinless chicken thighs, cut into bite size pieces
- 250g closed cup mushrooms, sliced
- 2 leeks, finely sliced

- 1 tbsp dried thyme
- 3 tbsp soft butter, divided
- 2 tbsp plain flour
- 500ml chicken stock
- 150ml double cream

For brushing:

- 1 egg beaten and mixed with tbsp water

METHOD

1. In a bowl, add flour, butter, salt and rub with hands until it's like breadcrumbs. Add the water 2 tablespoons at a time, mix then bring together in a ball. Divide into two equal portions. Cover with cling film and refrigerate.

2. Flip the SmartSwitch to AIR FRY/HOB. Select SEAR/SAUTÉ and set to 4 . Press START/STOP to begin cooking. Add 1 tbsp butter , then add leeks. Cook until soft. Then add the chicken and cook until no pink colour remains. Add the mushroom and cook until all the liquid absorbed. Press START/STOP to stop cooking. Transfer to a bowl.

3. Add the remaining butter, thyme and the flour into the cooking pot and stir until combined. Add the chicken stock, and double cream while whisking, simmer until thickened. Add the chicken/mushroom mixture into the pot. Stir and press START/STOP to stop cooking.

4. On a lightly floured surface, roll out each pastry ball into 1-cm thick circle. Press the circle into a greased 20-cm deep tart tin. (or cut out sixteen 10-cm rounds, to line eight 10-cm tart tins).

5. Press the dough into the tin and fill with filling mixture. Cover the tin with a remaining pastry circle. Brush the top with egg/water mixture.

49

6. Add 300ml water to the pot. Push in the legs on the Cook & Crisp tray, then place the tray in the bottom position in the pot. Add the tart tin on the tray.

7. Close the lid and flip the SmartSwitch to RAPID COOKER. Select STEAM BAKE, set temperature to 180˚C and set time to 40 minutes. Select START/STOP to begin cooking.

8. When cooking is complete, remove from unit. Serve.

Roasted Chicken legs, Broccoli and Garlic Potato Mash

 *Serving Size:* 4    *Cooking Time:* 17 Minutes   £ *Cost Per Serving:* £1

INGREDIENTS

Bottom of pot:

- 600g potatoes, peeled and chopped
- 300ml water
- 1 tsp salt
- 400g small broccoli florets
- 2 garlic cloves, minced
- 20g butter, room temperature
- 50ml double cream

Tray:

- 1 kg chicken legs
- 2 tbsp oil
- 1 tsp smoked paprika
- 1 tbsp onion powder
- Salt and pepper to taste

METHOD

1. In a bowl add all tray ingredients and stir until all the chicken coated with oil and seasoning.

2. Add the water, potatoes, salt and garlic to the pot. Stir. Add the broccoli over the potatoes. Do Not Stir.

3. Pull out the legs on the Cook & Crisp tray, then place tray in the top position in the pot, above the broccoli. Place the chicken on top of the tray.

4. Close the lid and flip the SmartSwitch to RAPID COOKER. Select SPEEDI MEALS, set temperature to 190˚ C and set time to 17 minutes. Select START/STOP to begin cooking.

5. When cooking is complete, open lid and transfer chicken to a serving plate. Then use silicone-tipped tongs to grab the centre handle and remove the tray from the unit. Transfer the broccoli to the serving plate with the chicken.

6. Transfer the potatoes to a bowl, mash the potato and add the double cream and butter. Mix. Serve the chicken legs with broccoli and potato mash.

51

Garlic Chicken Wings and Cheesy Pasta

 **Serving Size:** 4    **Cooking Time:** 15 Minutes   £ **Cost Per Serving:** £1

INGREDIENTS

Bottom of pot:
- 300g spirali pasta
- 120ml double cream
- 300ml milk
- 200ml water
- 200g cheddar cheese
- 3 tbsp butter
- ½ tsp garlic powder
- 1 tsp smoked paprika
- ½ tsp onion powder
- Salt and pepper to taste

Tray:
- 1 kg chicken wings
- 2 tsp oil
- 2 tbsp cornflour
- 4 garlic cloves, minced
- 2 tsp smoked paprika
- Salt and pepper to taste

METHOD

1. In a bowl, add chicken wings, oil, cornflour, garlic, paprika, salt, pepper and mix.

2. Add all the pot ingredients to the Ninja Speedi Cooking pot.

3. Pull out the legs on the Cook & Crisp tray, then place tray in the top position in the pot. Place the chicken wings on top of the tray.

4. Close the lid and flip the SmartSwitch to RAPID COOKER. Select SPEEDI MEALS, set temperature to 190˚ C and set time to 15 minutes. Select START/STOP to begin cooking.

5. When cooking is complete, transfer chicken to a plate. Then use silicone-tipped tongs to grab the centre handle and remove the tray from the unit. Stir pasta and serve with chicken wings.

53

Stuffed Chicken Breast and Rice

 *Serving Size:* 4  *Cooking Time:* 15 Minutes £ *Cost Per Serving:* £1.30

INGREDIENTS

Bottom of pot:

- 400g long grain rice
- 800ml stock or water
- 1 tsp salt
- 20g butter

Tray:

- 4 boneless, skinless chicken breasts
- 2 tbs oil
- 200g spinach

- 1 medium onion, finely chopped
- ½ tsp dried oregano
- 2 cloves garlic, minced
- 30g grated Parmigiano Reggiano
- 200g pizza sauce/pizza topper
- 20g butter

METHOD

1. Flip the SmartSwitch to AIR FRY/HOB. Select SEAR/SAUTÉ and set to 3 Press START/STOP to begin. Add oil to the pot, add the garlic, spinach, oregano and onion. Cook, stirring until it wilts.Select START/STOP to stop cooking. Add the Parmigiano, season with salt, pepper and stir. Set aside.

2. On a chopping board, lay the chicken breast. Insert the tip of a sharp knife into the center of the thickest part of the breast and then make a pocket in the breast. Do not cut all the way through. Repeat with the remaining breasts.

3. Season each breast with salt and pepper. Then fill the pockets with the spinach mixture. Secure each pocket using a toothpick.

4. Add the rice, butter and stock the pot. Season with salt and stir. Pull out the legs on the Cook & Crisp tray, then place tray in the top position in the pot, above the rice. Arrange the chicken breasts on the tray.

5. Close the lid and flip the SmartSwitch to RAPID COOKER. Select SPEEDI MEALS, set temperature to 200° C and set time to 15 minutes. Select START/STOP to begin cooking.

6. When time reaches 13 minutes, oped lid brush the chicken breasts with pizza sauce/topper, close lid to continue cooking.
   When cooking is complete, open lid, transfer chicken to serving plates, stir rice and serve with the stuffed chicken breasts with more pizza sauce/topper if desired. (If the rice needs more time, switch to SEAR/SAUTÉ and cook with the lid open until liquid is absorbed.

53

Chicken and Cauliflower Bake

 *Serving Size:* 6    *Cooking Time:* 24 Minutes   £ *Cost Per Serving:* £1..4

INGREDIENTS

- 1 cauliflower, cut into florets
- 1 large onion , chopped
- 1 garlic clove, minced
- 8 boneless, skinless chicken thighs, cut into bite size pieces
- 2 tsp tomato puree
- 1 tbsp smoked paprika
- ½ tsp chilli powder

- 3 tbsp oil
- 300ml chicken stock or water
- Salt and pepper to taste

METHOD

1. Flip the SmartSwitch to AIR FRY/HOB. Select SEAR/SAUTÉ and set to 4 . Press START/STOP to begin cooking. Add the oil to the pot. Add the onions and garlic to the pot and saute until softened. Press START/STOP to turn off the SEAR/SAUTÉ function. Add all ingredients to the pot and stir.

2. Close the lid and flip the SmartSwitch to RAPID COOKER. Select STEAM AIR FRY and set the temperature to 180° C and time to 24 minutes. Select START/STOP to begin cooking.

3. When cooking is complete, open lid and serve .

Chicken And Courgette Soup

 *Serving Size:* 4

 *Cooking Time:* 15 Minutes

£ *Cost Per Serving:* 70p

INGREDIENTS

- 1 tbsp oil
- 2 skinless, boneless chicken breasts, cut into bite size pieces
- 2 large courgettes , chopped
- 1 small carrot, cut into small cubes
- 1 medium onion, chopped
- 2 celery stalks, chopped
- 2 garlic cloves, minced
- 1 tbsp dried thyme
- 1 litre chicken stock
- Salt and pepper to taste

METHOD

1. Flip the SmartSwitch to AIR FRY/HOB. Select SEAR/SAUTÉ and set to 3 . Press START/STOP to begin cooking. Add the oil, chicken and brown on all sides. Add onion, garlic and celery. Cook until soft.Press START/STOP to stop cooking.

2. Add all remaining ingredients to the Ninja Speedi and stir.

3. Close the lid and flip the SmartSwitch to RAPID COOKER. Select STEAM BAKE and set the temperature to 180° C and time to 15 minutes. Select START/STOP to begin cooking.

4. When cooking is complete, open lid, adjust seasoning, stir and serve .

Chicken and Chickpea Tikka Masala

 **Serving Size**: 6    **Cooking Time**: 25 Minutes    **Cost Per Serving**: £1.5

INGREDIENTS

- 6 bone in, skin on chicken thighs and drumsticks
- 30g butter
- 1 tbsp ground cumin
- 1 tsp ground ginger
- 1 tbsp smoked paprika
- 3/4 tsp ground turmeric
- 1 medium onion, finely chopped
- 3 garlic cloves , minced
- 1 (400g) tin chopped tomatoes
- 250ml chicken stock
- 1 (400g) tin chickpeas, drained
- 120ml double cream
- Salt and pepper to taste

METHOD

1. Flip the SmartSwitch to AIR FRY/HOB. Select SEAR/SAUTÉ and set to 3 . Press START/STOP to begin cooking. Add the butter to the pot. Add the onions, spices and garlic to the pot and saute until softened. Add the tomatoes and double cream. Cook for 2 minutes. Press START/STOP to turn off the SEAR/SAUTÉ function. Add the chicken, stock and chickpeas into the pot, stir.

2. Close the lid and flip the SmartSwitch to RAPID COOKER. Select STEAM BAKE and set the temperature to 180° C and time to 25 minutes. Select START/STOP to begin cooking.

3. When cooking is complete, open lid and serve .

Turkey and Potato Stew

 *Serving Size: 4*    *Cooking Time: 4 hours*   £ *Cost Per Serving: £1.40*

INGREDIENTS

- 500g skinless, boneless turkey breasts or thighs, cut into bite size pieces
- 600g baby potatoes, peeled and halved if large
- 1 small onion, chopped
- 2 cloves garlic, minced
- 1 tsp dried thyme
- 1.5 litre chicken stock
- 4 tbsp tomato puree
- Salt and pepper to taste

METHOD

1. Add the potatoes, onion, garlic, stock, thyme, tomato puree to Ninja Speedi pot. Stir, add the turkey pieces on top layer. Do Not Stir.

2. Close the lid, flip the SmartSwitch to AIR FRY/HOB, then use the centre arrows select SLOW COOK, set temperature to HIGH and time to 4 hours (or Low for 6 hours). Select START/STOP to begin cooking.

3. When cooking is complete, open lid and serve .

Whole garlic and Herbs Roasted Chicken

 **Serving Size:** 4

 **Cooking Time:** 50 mins

£ **Cost Per Serving:** 90p

INGREDIENTS

- 2kg whole chicken, room temperature
- 60ml melted unsalted butter
- 3 tbsp olive oil
- Juice and zest of 1 large lemon
- 8 garlic cloves, minced
- 3 rosemary sprigs or 1 tbsp dried rosemary
- 3 thyme springs or 1 tbsp dried thyme
- Salt and pepper to taste

METHOD

1. In a large bowl, add the oil, butter, lemon juice, zest, rosemary, thyme, salt and pepper. Mix and add the chicken and rub seasoning mixture over the chicken, under the skin and inside the cavity.

2. Add 500ml water into the cooking pot. Push in the legs on the Cook & Crisp tray, then place tray in the bottom position in the pot. Add the chicken on the tray.

3. Close the lid and flip the SmartSwitch to RAPID COOKER. Select STEAM AIR FRY, set temperature to 180° C and set time to 50 minutes. Select START/STOP to begin cooking.

4. When the cooking is complete, remove chicken from pot, cover loosely with foil and allow to rest for 10 minutes before serving.

Hunter's Chicken

 Serving Size: 5  Cooking Time: 40 mins £ Cost Per Serving: £1

INGREDIENTS

- 1 tbsp oil
- 1 kg chicken drumsticks
- 4 tbsp plain flour
- 1 large red bell pepper, sliced
- 1 onion, finely chopped
- 2 garlic cloves, minced
- 2 tsp tomato puree
- 250ml chicken stock
- 1 (400g) tin chopped tomatoes

- 1 bay leaf
- 45g black pitted olives
- Handful flat leaf parsley, chopped
- Salt and pepper to taste

METHOD

1. Coat the chicken drumsticks with flour.

2. Flip the SmartSwitch to AIR FRY/HOB. Select SEAR/SAUTÉ and set to 4 . Press START/STOP to begin cooking. Add the oil, chicken drumsticks and brown . Add onions and garlic and cook until soft . Press START/STOP to stop cooking. Add all ingredients to the cooking pot and stir.

3. Close the lid and flip the SmartSwitch to AIR FRY/HOB, then use the centre arrows to select BAKE/ROAST. Set temperature to 170˚ C and set time to 40 minutes. Select START/STOP to begin cooking.

4. When cooking is complete, open lid and stir. Transfer to serving plate and sprinkle with parsley. Serve with potato mash or crusty bread.

Chicken and Vegetable Sandwich

 *Serving Size:* 4

 *Cooking Time:* 9 Minutes

£ *Cost Per Serving:* 90p

INGREDIENTS

For the chicken:

- 4 small boneless, skinless chicken breasts
- 4 tsp balsamic vinegar
- 3 garlic cloves, minced
- 1 tsp dried thyme
- 2 tbsp oil
- Salt and pepper to taste

To assemble the sandwiches:

- 4 cheese slices
- lettuce
- tomatoes, chopped
- 4 crusty white thick bread slices

METHOD

1. In a bowl add chicken, vinegar, garlic, thyme, oil and stir until all the chicken coated with seasoning.

2. Pull out the legs on the Cook & Crisp tray, then place tray in the top position in the pot. Place the chicken on top of the tray.

3. Close the lid. Flip SmartSwitch to AIR FRY/HOB, then use the centre arrows to select GRILL. Set temperature to 220° C and set time to 9 minutes. Select START/STOP to begin cooking.

4. When time reaches 4 minutes, open lid and flip the chicken. Close lid to continue cooking.

5. When cooking is complete, use tongs to remove the chicken from the tray and transfer to a plate. Set aside for 5 minutes, then slice.

6. Slice each bread slice in half and fill with the vegetables, slice of cheese and chicken slices and serve.

Chicken and Mushroom Risotto

 *Serving Size*: 4　　 *Cooking Time*: 15 Minutes　　£ *Cost Per Serving*: £1.80

INGREDIENTS

- 2 tbsp oil
- 500g boneless, skinless chicken thigh, cut into 3-cm pieces
- 1 onion, finely chopped
- 4 garlic cloves, minced
- 250g closed cup mushrooms, sliced
- 400g Arborio risotto rice
- 1 litre chicken stock
- 30g grated Parmigiano Reggiano
- 50g unsalted butter
- Salt and pepper to taste

METHOD

1. Flip the SmartSwitch to AIR FRY/HOB. Select SEAR/SAUTÉ and set to 4 . Press START/STOP to begin cooking. Add the oil to the pot. Add the onion. Cook until soft. Add chicken and brown on all sides. Select START/STOP to stop cooking.

2. Place the stock, rice, mushroom, garlic, pepper and salt in the Ninja Speedi Pot, stir.

3. Close the lid and flip the SmartSwitch to RAPID COOKER. Select STEAM BAKE and set the temperature to 190° C and time to 15 minutes. Select START/STOP to begin cooking.

4. When cooking is complete, open lid, add the cheese and butter and stir to combine. If the mixture is too thick, stir in 60ml chicken stock.
Serve warm.

Chicken and Creamy Pasta

 **Serving Size:** 4    **Cooking Time:** 15 Minutes   £ **Cost Per Serving:** £1.40

INGREDIENTS

Tray:

- 4 (180g each) chicken breasts
- 1 tbsp garlic powder
- 1 tbsp onion powder
- 1 tsp dried oregano
- 1 tsp dried rosemary
- 2 tbsp oil
- Salt and pepper to taste

Bottom of the pot:

- 225g Linguine pasta, split in half
- 1 garlic clove, minced
- 500ml water
- 250ml double cream
- 40g butter, cut into pieces
- 30g grated Parmigiano Reggiano
- Salt and pepper to taste

METHOD

1. In a bowl add chicken breasts, garlic powder, onion powder, oregano, rosemary, salt, pepper, oil and mix until all the chicken coated with seasoning.

2. Place all the creamy pasta ingredients in the Ninja Speedi Pot, stir (make sure that the pasta is covered by liquid).

3. Pull out the legs on the Cook & Crisp tray, then place tray in the top position in the pot. Place the chicken breasts on top of the tray.

4. Close the lid and flip the SmartSwitch to RAPID COOKER. Select SPEEDI MEALS and set the temperature to 190° C and time to 15 minutes. Select START/STOP to begin cooking.

5. When time reaches 5 minutes, open lid and flip the chicken. Close lid to continue cooking.

6. When cooking is complete, use tongs to remove the chicken from the tray and transfer to a plate. Set aside for 5 minutes, then slice.
   Let the pasta set for 5 minutes, then Stir pasta and serve with chicken.

62

Tuna Lemon Spaghetti

 **Serving Size:** *3-4*    **Cooking Time:** *10 Minutes*   **£** **Cost Per Serving:** *40p*

INGREDIENTS

- 300g spaghetti pasta, split in half
- 2 tbsp oil
- 800ml water
- 3 (145g each) tins tuna chunks, drained
- Juice and zest of 1 lemon
- Salt and pepper to taste

METHOD

1. Add the water, spaghetti, oil the pot. Season with salt and stir.

2. Close the lid and flip the SmartSwitch to RAPID COOKER. Select STEAM, set time to 10 minutes. Select START/STOP to begin cooking.

3. In a bowl, add the drained tuna, lemon juice, zest, salt and pepper. Stir.

4. When cooking is complete, open lid and add the tuna mixture. Stir and let sit for 5 minutes, then serve.

Salmon and Rice Cakes

 *Serving Size:* 4    *Cooking Time:* 8 Minutes   £ *Cost Per Serving:* 60p

INGREDIENTS

- 400g tinned salmon, drained
- 400g cooked rice
- 2 small eggs
- 3 tbsp breadcrumbs
- 1 green onion, finely chopped
- Salt and pepper to taste

METHOD

1. In a bowl add all ingredients and mix until combined. Shape into 6 equal balls and then flatten slightly.

2. Push in the legs on the Cook & Crisp tray, then place tray in the bottom position in the pot. Place the salmon rice cakes on top of the tray, brush with oil.

3. Close the lid and flip the SmartSwitch to AIR FRY/HOB, then use the centre arrows to select AIR FRY. Set temperature to 200° C and set time to 8 minutes. Select START/STOP to begin cooking.

4. When time reaches 4 minutes, flip the salmon cakes. Close lid to continue cooking.

5. When cooking is complete, open lid and use tongs to remove from the Ninja Speedi and serve.

Fish Burgers

 *Serving Size: 4*  *Cooking Time: 15 Minutes* £ *Cost Per Serving: £1*

INGREDIENTS

- 350g frozen cod fillets, defrosted
- 3 tbsp plain flour
- 1 egg
- 75g breadcrumbs
- Salt and pepper to taste

METHOD

1. Trim each cod fillet and shape into square.

2. In a bowl, add flour and salt. In a second bowl add the egg and whisk. In a third bowl, add the breadcrumbs and season with salt and pepper.

3. Coat the fish in flour, then dip in the egg, then finally coat in breadcrumbs.

4. Push in the legs on the Cook & Crisp tray, then place tray in the bottom position in the pot. Place the fish burgers on top of the tray, brush with oil.

5. Close the lid and flip the SmartSwitch to AIR FRY/HOB, then use the centre arrows to select AIR FRY. Set temperature to 170° C and set time to 15 minutes. Select START/STOP to begin cooking.

6. When time reaches 7 minutes, open lid and flip the burgers. Close lid to continue cooking. When cooking is complete, open lid and serve in bread with tomatoes slices and lettuce .

65

Fish Curry

 **Serving Size:** 4    **Cooking Time:** 15 Minutes   £ **Cost Per Serving:** £1

INGREDIENTS

- 500g white fish (Hake, basa or cod) fillets, cut into 5-cm cubes
- 1 onion, chopped
- 2 garlic cloves, minced
- 2 tbsp curry powder
- 1 tbsp tomato puree
- 400ml tin chopped tomatoes
- 400ml tin coconut milk
- 1 bell red pepper, finely chopped
- 1 bell green pepper, finely chopped
- Salt and pepper to taste

METHOD

1. Add all ingredients (except fish) into the Ninja Speedi cooking pot, and stir. Place the fish fillets on top of the sauce mixture.

2. Close the lid and flip the SmartSwitch to RAPID COOKER. Select STEAM BAKE and set temperature to 190° C and time to 15 minutes. Select START/STOP to begin cooking.

3. When cooking is complete, open lid and serve with rice.

Baked Fish with Broccoli and Cheddar

 *Serving Size: 4*    *Cooking Time: 20 Minutes*    *Cost Per Serving: £ 1.5*

INGREDIENTS

- 500g white fish (Hake, basa or cod) fillets, cut into 5-cm cubes
- 200g broccoli, cut into small florets
- 300ml single cream
- 200ml vegetable stock
- 2 garlic cloves, minced
- 150g grated cheddar cheese
- Salt and pepper to taste

METHOD

1. Add all ingredients into the cooking pot and stir.

2. Close the lid and flip the SmartSwitch to AIR FRY/HOB, then use the centre arrows to select BAKE/ROAST. Set temperature to 180° C and set time to 20 minutes. Select START/STOP to begin cooking.

3. When cooking is complete, open lid, transfer to a plate, and serve.

Salmon Pasta with Garden Peas

 *Serving Size:* 4    *Cooking Time:* 15 Minutes   £ *Cost Per Serving:* £ 1.1

INGREDIENTS

- 1 tbsp oil
- 1 garlic clove, minced
- 375g frozen garden peas
- 400g tinned salmon, drained
- 500g Linguine pasta, broken in half
- 1 litre water
- Salt and pepper to taste

METHOD

1. Add all ingredients into the cooking pot (except salmon) and stir.

2. Close the lid and flip the SmartSwitch to RAPID COOKER. Select SPEEDI MEALS, set temperature to 190° C and set time to 15 minutes. Select START/STOP to begin cooking.

3. When cooking is complete, open lid, add the tinned salmon and stir let set for 5 minutes. transfer to a plate, and serve.

Haddock Bake

 Serving Size: 4   Cooking Time: 23 Minutes   £ Cost Per Serving: £1.30

INGREDIENTS

- 300g skinless & boneless haddock fillets, cut into 4-cm chunks
- 500g Maris Piper potatoes, peeled and sliced into ½-cm thick slices
- 225g frozen garden peas
- 1 tsp dried thyme
- 1 leek, sliced
- 200ml vegetable stock
- 100g grated cheddar
- Salt and pepper to taste

METHOD

1. Grease 20-cm deep baking dish. Add the fish chunks into the prepared dish and top with leek slices and frozen peas. Season with thyme, salt and pepper. Arrange the potato slices over the fish mixture. Pour in the stock and sprinkle with cheese and more salt and pepper. Cover with tin foil.

2. Push in the legs on the Cook & Crisp tray, then place the tray in the bottom position in the pot. Place the dish on the tray.

3. Close the lid and flip the SmartSwitch to AIR FRY/HOB, then use the centre arrows to select BAKE/ROAST. Set temperature to 170˚ C and set time to 35 minutes. Select START/STOP to begin cooking.

4. When cooking is complete, remove the tin foil. Close the lid and flip the SmartSwitch to AIR FRY/HOB, then use the centre arrows to select BAKE/ROAST. Set temperature to 190˚ C and set time to 10 minutes. Select START/STOP to begin cooking.

5. When cooking is complete, remove from unit and let stand 5 minutes before serving.

Roasted Prawns and Orzo

 *Serving Size:* 4

 *Cooking Time:* 5 Minutes

£ *Cost Per Serving:* £1.70

INGREDIENTS

- 1 tsp oil
- 2 tbsp butter
- 450g orzo pasta
- 1.2 litre vegetable or chicken stock
- Handful fresh or frozen spinach, defrosted and drained
- 225g raw frozen prawns, defrosted and peeled
- 1 medium onion, finely chopped

- 2 garlic cloves, minced
- Zest and juice of one medium lemon
- 50g sun-dried tomatoes, chopped (optional)
- Salt and pepper to taste
- Handful chopped flat leaf parsley

METHOD

1. Flip the SmartSwitch to AIR FRY/HOB. Select SEAR/SAUTÉ and set to 4 . Press START/STOP to begin cooking. Add the oil to the pot. Add the onion. Cook until soft. Add garlic and cook for a minute. Select START/STOP to stop cooking.

2. Place the orzo, stock, spinach, sun-dried tomatoes (if using) , and salt in the pot and stir to combine.

3. Push in the legs on the Cook & Crisp tray, then place the tray in the bottom position in the pot. Place the prawns on the tray, season with salt and pepper.

4. Close the lid and flip the SmartSwitch to RAPID COOKER. Select SPEEDI MEALS and set the temperature to 200° C and time to 5 minutes. Select START/STOP to begin cooking.

5. When cooking is complete, open lid, transfer the prawns into a plate. Then use silicone-tipped tongs to grab the centre handle and remove the tray from the unit. Stir orzo, add the butter, lemon juice, zest and stir again and serve with roasted prawns.

70

Tomato Poached Fish Fillets

 *Serving Size: 4*    *Cooking Time: 15 Minutes*   £ *Cost Per Serving: £1*

INGREDIENTS

- 600g white fish fillet
- 1 tbsp oil
- 1 small onion, finely chopped
- 3 garlic cloves, minced
- ½ tsp dried oregano
- 1 (400g) tin chopped tomatoes
- 150g baby tomatoes, or regular tomatoes, chopped
- Salt and pepper to taste

METHOD

1. Flip the SmartSwitch to AIR FRY/HOB. Select SEAR/SAUTÉ and set to 4 . Press START/STOP to begin cooking. Add the oil to the pot. Add the onion. Cook until soft. Add garlic and cook for a minute. Select START/STOP to stop cooking.

2. Place the chopped tomatoes, baby tomatoes, oregano, salt and pepper in the pot and stir to combine.

3. Season the fish fillets on both sides with salt and pepper. Place the fish fillets on top of tomato mixture into the pot.

4. Close the lid and flip the SmartSwitch to RAPID COOKER. Select STEAM BAKE and set the temperature to 190° C and time to 15 minutes. Select START/STOP to begin cooking.

5. When cooking is complete, transfer into a plate and serve.

Fish Fingers and Mushy Peas

 *Serving Size: 4*    *Cooking Time: 8 Minutes*    *Cost Per Serving: £1*

INGREDIENTS

- 4 large white fillets, defrosted and cut into 3-cm wide fingers
- 5 tbsp plain flour
- 70g breadcrumbs
- 2 large eggs
- Salt and pepper to taste

For the mushy peas:
- 400g frozen garden peas
- 1 small onion, finely chopped
- 2 garlic cloves, minced
- Zest of 1 small lemon
- 200ml water
- Salt and pepper to taste

METHOD

1. In a shallow bowl add flour, salt, pepper and mix, in another shallow bowl add egg and whisk, and add breadcrumbs in a third shallow bowl.

2. Press the fish fingers into flour, then in the beaten egg, and in breadcrumbs.

3. Place the peas, water, onion , garlic, zest, salt, and pepper to cooking pot. Stir.

4. Push in the legs on the Cook & Crisp tray, then place the tray in the bottom position in the pot. Place the fish fingers on the tray.

5. Close the lid and flip the SmartSwitch to RAPID COOKER. Select STEAM AIR FRY and set the temperature to 200° C and time to 8 minutes. Select START/STOP to begin cooking.

6. When time reaches 4 minutes, open lid, flip the fish fingers using silicone-tipped tongs. Close lid to continue cooking.

7. When cooking is complete, open lid, transfer the fish fingers into a plate. Then use silicone-tipped tongs to grab the centre handle and remove the tray from the unit. Mash the peas with a fork. Serve fish fingers with mashed peas.

This Fish Fingers are guaranteed to be a crowd pleaser, especially the kids. These are a simple, and delicious, served with mushy peas. Perfect for a lunch with family or friends.

Prawn Curry

 *Serving Size:* 4    *Cooking Time:* 5 Minutes   £ *Cost Per Serving:* £2.30

INGREDIENTS

- 500g peeled raw king prawns, defrosted
- 1 tsp oil
- 1 onion, finely chopped
- 4 garlic cloves, minced
- 1 tsp ground turmeric
- ½ tsp garam masala
- 1 (400g) tin chopped tomatoes
- 100ml water
- 2 tsp tomato puree
- 150ml single cream
- Salt and pepper to taste

METHOD

1. Flip the SmartSwitch to AIR FRY/HOB. Select SEAR/SAUTÉ and set to 4 . Press START/STOP to begin cooking. Add the oil to the pot. Add the onion. Cook until soft. Add garlic, all of the spices and stir for a minute. Add the chopped tomato, water and simmer for 5 minutes. Select START/STOP to stop cooking.

2. Add the prawns and stir. Close the lid and flip the SmartSwitch to RAPID COOKER. Select STEAM BAKE and set the temperature to 190˚ C and time to 5 minutes. Select START/STOP to begin cooking.

3. When cooking is complete, add the single cream, adjust seasoning, stir and serve with rice.

Aubergine Parmigiana

 *Serving Size:* 4   *Cooking Time:* 35 Minutes   £ *Cost Per Serving:* £1.20

INGREDIENTS

- 500g aubergine, sliced into 2-cm thick lengthways
- 2 tbsp oil
- 1 (400g) tin chopped tomatoes
- 150ml water
- 6 tbsp tomato puree
- 4 basil leaves
- 2 garlic cloves, minced
- 50g grated Parmigiano Reggiano
- 200g grated Mozzarella
- Salt and pepper to taste

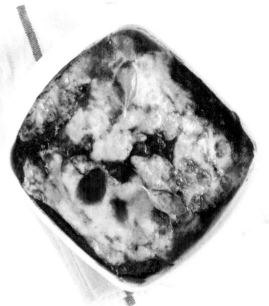

METHOD

1. Pull out the legs on the Cook & Crisp tray, then place tray in the top position in the pot. Arrange the aubergine slices on the tray, then brush with oil. (you may need to work in batches)

2. Close the lid and flip the SmartSwitch to AIR FRY/HOB, then use the centre arrows to select BAKE/ROAST. Set temperature to 160° C and set time to 8 minutes. Select START/STOP to begin cooking.

3. When cooking is complete, open lid, transfer aubergines to a plate. Flip the SmartSwitch to AIR FRY/HOB. Select SEAR/SAUTÉ and set to 4 . Press START/STOP to begin cooking. Add the oil to the pot. Add the garlic, tomato puree, chopped tomato, basil, water, salt and pepper. Cook, stirring occasionally until thickened sightly for about 5 minutes. Select START/STOP to stop cooking.

4. Grease an oven proof dish that will fit in your Ninja Speedi. Spoon some of the tomato sauce in the dish, spread the sauce, top with a layer of aubergine slices and sprinkle with mozzarella cheese. Repeat layering (tomato sauce, aubergine, mozzarella, tomato sauce) and finally top with grated Parmigiano Reggiano.

5. Push in the legs on the Cook & Crisp tray, then place the tray in the bottom position in the pot.

6. Close the lid and flip the SmartSwitch to AIR FRY/HOB, then use the centre arrows to select BAKE/ROAST. Set temperature to 160° C and set time to 15 minutes. Select START/STOP to begin cooking.

7. When cooking is complete, open lid, transfer to serving plates, and serve with bread.

75

Cheese and Onion Pasties

 *Serving Size: 4*

 Cooking Time: 30 Minutes

£ *Cost Per Serving: £75p*

INGREDIENTS

For the pastry:

- 300g plain flour
- 150g cold butter, cut into small cubes
- 1 medium egg
- Cold milk, as needed
- Pinch of salt

For brushing:

- 1 egg, beaten

For the filling:

- 40g butter
- 1 onion, finely chopped
- 250g Maris Piper potatoes, cut into 1-cm cubes
- 150g mature grated cheddar
- 3 tbsp double cream

METHOD

1. In a bowl, add flour, butter, salt and rub with hands until it's like breadcrumbs. Add the egg and cold milk (2 tablespoons at a time), mix then bring together in a ball (if its too dry add more milk, 1 tbsp at a time). Divide pastry into 4 equal portions. Cover with cling film and refrigerate.

2. Flip the SmartSwitch to AIR FRY/HOB. Select SEAR/SAUTÉ and set to 4 . Press START/STOP to begin cooking. Add the butter to the pot. Add the onion. Cook, stirring occasionally until soft. Add the potatoes and cook for 4 minutes. Select START/STOP to stop cooking. Transfer into a bowl and set aside to cool.

3. On a lightly floured surface, roll out each pastry portion into ½-cm thick circle. Set aside.

4. Add the cheese and cream into potato/onion mixture, season with salt and pepper and stir.

5. Add ¼ of the filling mixture into one half of each pastry, leaving some space around around the edge. Brush the edge with beaten egg. Fold the empty pastry half over the filling and seal the edges. Brush the tops with the beaten egg.

6. Push in the legs on the Cook & Crisp tray, then place the tray in the bottom position in the pot. Arrange the pasties on the tray.

7. Close the lid and flip the SmartSwitch to AIR FRY/HOB, then use the centre arrows to select BAKE/ROAST. Set temperature to 170˚ C and set time to 30 minutes. Select START/STOP to begin cooking.
   When cooking is complete, open lid, serve hot.

76

Rice with Aubergine and Mushrooms

 *Serving Size:* 4    *Cooking Time:* 10 Minutes   £ *Cost Per Serving:* 86p

INGREDIENTS

- 400g basmati or long-grain rice
- 800ml water or stock
- 200g mushroom, chopped
- 1 onion, chopped
- 3 garlic cloves, minced
- 1 small carrot, grated
- 1 tsp ground cumin
- 1 tsp paprika
- 500g aubergine, cut into cubes
- 2 tbsp oil
- 3 tbsp tomato puree
- Salt and pepper to taste

METHOD

1. Flip the SmartSwitch to AIR FRY/HOB. Select SEAR/SAUTÉ and set to 4 . Press START/STOP to begin cooking. Add the oil to the pot. Add the onion, and garlic. Cook, stirring occasionally for about 3 minutes. Select START/STOP to stop cooking.

2. Add all ingredients and stir.

3. Close the lid and flip the SmartSwitch to RAPID COOKER. Select STEAM BAKE and set the temperature to 190° C and time to 10 minutes. Select START/STOP to begin cooking.

4. When cooking is complete, open lid, fluff the rice with a fork, and serve.

Potato Curry

 *Serving Size: 4*  *Cooking Time: 15 Minutes*  *Cost Per Serving: 50p*

INGREDIENTS

- 2 tbsp oil
- 300g potatoes, peeled and chopped into 2-cm cubes
- 1 onion, finely chopped
- 2 cloves garlic, minced
- 1 tsp ginger powder
- 1 tsp turmeric powder
- 1 tsp ground coriander

- 1 tsp smoked paprika
- 1 tsp garam masala
- 1 (400g) tin chopped tomatoes
- 240ml vegetable or chicken stock
- Salt and pepper to taste

METHOD

1. Flip the SmartSwitch to AIR FRY/HOB. Select SEAR/SAUTÉ and set to 4 . Press START/STOP to begin cooking. Add the oil to the pot. Add the onion. Cook until soft. Add the garlic and all the spices and cook for a minute. Select START/STOP to stop cooking.

2. Add all remaining ingredients into the pot. Stir.

3. Close the lid and flip the SmartSwitch to RAPID COOKER. Select STEAM AIR FRY and set the temperature to 200° C and time to 15 minutes. Select START/STOP to begin cooking.

4. When cooking is complete, open lid, transfer into a serving dish. Serve with rice or bread.

This Potato Curry is a simple, hearty, comfortable and suitable for a filling family meal or a special supper.

Feta Pasta

Serving Size: 4

Cooking Time: 16 Minutes

Cost Per Serving: £1

INGREDIENTS

Tray:

- 250g block feta cheese
- 400g baby tomatoes
- 30ml olive oil
- 4 garlic cloves, minced
- 1 tsp oregano or thy

Bottom of the pot:

- 1 tsp oil
- 350g penne pasta
- 700ml water

METHOD

1. Place the feta cheese block in the center of Multi-Purpose Tin or 20-cm cake tin, Add the baby tomatoes around the cheese. Pour the olive oil over the cheese and tomatoes, season with salt and pepper.

2. Place the pasta, water, oil and salt in the Ninja Speedi Pot, stir.

3. Pull out the legs on the Cook & Crisp tray, then place tray in the top position in the pot, above the pasta. Place the tin on top of the tray.

4. Close the lid and flip the SmartSwitch to RAPID COOKER. Select SPEEDI MEALS and set the temperature to 190˚ C and time to 16 minutes. Select START/STOP to begin cooking.

5. When cooking is complete, open lid and remove the tin. Then use silicone-tipped tongs to grab the centre handle and remove the tray from the unit.

6. Using a fork, mash the cheese and tomatoes. Add the minced garlic and stir. Stir the pasta and add the tomato/cheese mixture into the pot. Close the lid and let set for 3 minutes.
Serve.

Vegetable Stew

 *Serving Size: 4*    *Cooking Time: 15 Minutes*   £ *Cost Per Serving: 80p*

INGREDIENTS

- 1 tsp oil
- 300g potato , peeled and cut into 2-cm cubes
- 300g aubergine , chopped
- 300g courgette, cut into pieces
- 1 large onion, chopped
- 2 garlic cloves, minced

- 1 (400g) tin chopped tomatoes
- 2 tbsp tomato puree
- 200ml water
- 2 tsp Worcestershire sauce
- Salt and pepper to taste

METHOD

1. Flip the SmartSwitch to AIR FRY/HOB. Select SEAR/SAUTÉ and set to 4 . Press START/STOP to begin cooking. Add the oil to the pot. Add the onion. Cook until soft. Add garlic and stir for a minute. Add all remaining ingredients and stir.

2. Close the lid and flip the SmartSwitch to RAPID COOKER. Select STEAM BAKE and set the temperature to 190° C and time to 15 minutes. Select START/STOP to begin cooking.

3. When cooking is complete, serve immediately

Potato and Mushroom Bake

 *Serving Size: 6*　　 *Cooking Time: 50 Minutes*　　 *Cost Per Serving: £1*

INGREDIENTS

- 300g closed cup mushrooms, sliced
- 1 kg Maris Piper or King Edward potatoes, peeled and thinly sliced
- 300ml double cream
- 350ml milk
- 2 tbsp dried rosemary
- 100g grated Cheddar
- Salt and pepper to taste

METHOD

1. Grease 20-cm deep pie dish and layer with potato slices, then top with a layer of mushroom and finally a sprinkle of cheese. Continue layering until all ingredients used up.

2. In a large bowl, add double cream, milk, rosemary, salt and pepper. Whisk until combined. Pour into the dish over the potatoes and mushroom. Top with grated cheese.

3. Push in the legs on the Cook & Crisp tray, then place the tray in the bottom position in the pot. Place the dish on the tray.

4. Close the lid and flip the SmartSwitch to AIR FRY/HOB, then use the centre arrows to select BAKE/ROAST. Set temperature to 180° C and set time to 50 minutes until cooked through . Select START/STOP to begin cooking.

5. When cooking is complete, serve immediately

Cauliflower Cheese

 Serving Size: 6　　 Cooking Time: 30 Minutes　　£ Cost Per Serving: 80p

INGREDIENTS

- 600g frozen cauliflower florets, defrosted and drained
- 1 tbsp oil
- 5 tbsp butter
- 4 tbsp plain flour
- 400ml milk
- 400ml double cream

- 200g grated mature Cheddar
- 1 tsp English mustard
- Salt and pepper to taste

METHOD

1. Flip the SmartSwitch to AIR FRY/HOB. Select SEAR/SAUTÉ and set to "3". Press START/STOP to begin cooking.

2. Add the flour, butter to the pot and cook, stirring regularly, for 3 minutes. Add milk and cream while whisking. Whisk until thick and creamy. Select START/STOP to stop cooking. Add 100g cheddar and mustard to sauce. Whisk until cheese melted, season with salt and pepper.

3. Add cauliflower and stir to coat in the sauce. Sprinkle with remaining cheese.

4. Close the lid and flip the SmartSwitch to AIR FRY/HOB, then use the centre arrows to select BAKE/ROAST. Set temperature to 170° C and time to 30 minutes. Select START/STOP to begin cooking.

5. When cooking is complete, open lid. Let stand 5 minutes then serve.

Butternut Squash and Bean Stew

 *Serving Size:* 4    *Cooking Time:* 35 Minutes   £ *Cost Per Serving:* 80p

INGREDIENTS

- 600g butternut squash peeled and cut into 2-cm pieces
- 1 tbsp oil
- 1 tbsp butter
- 1 large onion, chopped
- 3 garlic cloves, minced
- 2 (400g) tins chopped tomatoes

- 200ml chicken or vegetable stock
- 1 tsp ground cumin
- 1 tsp paprika
- 2 (400g each) butter beans In water, drained
- Salt and pepper to taste

METHOD

1. In a bowl, add the butternut squash pieces, oil, salt and pepper. Mix until squash coated with oil and seasoning.

2. Push in the legs on the Cook & Crisp tray, then place the tray in the bottom position in the pot. Arrange the squash on the tray.

3. Close the lid and flip the SmartSwitch to AIR FRY/HOB, then use the centre arrows to select BAKE/ROAST. Set temperature to 190° C and time to 15 minutes. Select START/STOP to begin cooking.

4. When cooking is complete, open lid. Transfer the squash into a plate. Then use silicone-tipped tongs to grab the centre handle and remove the tray from the unit.

5. Flip the SmartSwitch to AIR FRY/HOB. Select SEAR/SAUTÉ and set to "4". Press START/STOP to begin cooking. Add the butter to the pot. Add the onion. Cook until soft. Add garlic and stir for a minute. Place back the squash into the pot, add all remaining ingredients and stir. Select START/STOP to stop cooking.

6. Close the lid and flip the SmartSwitch to RAPID COOKER. Select STEAM BAKE and set temperature to 200° C, and time to 20 minutes. Select START/STOP to begin cooking.
   When cooking is complete, open lid, and stir. Serve with flatbread.

84

AFTERNOON TEA

Classic Afternoon Tea Recipes for a Proper British Tea Party

Pear Honey Cake

 *Serving Size: 8*    *Cooking Time: 45 Minutes*   £ *Cost Per Serving: 36p*

INGREDIENTS

- 220g plain flour
- 1 tsp baking powder
- ½ tsp bicarbonate of soda
- 180g unsalted butter, softened
- 120g caster sugar
- 2 large eggs
- 120ml milk

- Pinch of salt
- 1 tsp vanilla essence
- 300g ripe pears, peel and cut into slightly thick slices
- 1 tbsp brown sugar
- 2 tbsp runny honey

METHOD

1. In a bowl, add flour, baking powder, bicarbonate of soda, salt. Mix until combined.

2. In another bowl, add the butter, sugar and beat together until creamy. Add one egg while beating, then add one third of flour mixture and beat until combined. Add remaining eggs, flour, milk and vanilla, mix until combined.

3. Grease Multi-Purpose Tin or 20-cm cake tin and line with baking paper, transfer cake batter into the prepared tin.

4. Layer the pear slices on top of the cake. Sprinkle with brown sugar.

5. Add 500ml water to pot. Push in the legs on the Cook & Crisp tray, then place the tray in the bottom position in the pot. Place the tin on the tray.

6. Close the lid and flip the SmartSwitch to RAPID COOKER. Select STEAM BAKE and set time to 45 minutes and temperature to 160° C. Select START/STOP to begin cooking.

7. When cooking is complete, remove the cake tin from Speedi and let cool slightly, then brush the cake top with honey. Slice and serve.

86

Mini Orange Marmalade Cakes

 *Yield:* 12 Mini Cakes   *Cooking Time:* 30 Minutes   £ *Cost Per Serving:* 30p

INGREDIENTS

- 270g plain flour
- 1 tsp bicarbonate of soda
- 1 ½ tsp baking powder
- Pinch of salt
- 100g caster sugar
- 3 eggs
- 100g softened butter

- 100g natural Greek yogurt
- 200g orange marmalade
- 1 tsp vanilla essence

For brushing:
- 100g orange marmalade

METHOD

1. In a bowl, add flour, baking powder, bicarbonate of soda, salt. Mix until combined.

2. In another bowl, add the butter, sugar, eggs and beat together until creamy. Add flour mixture and beat until combined. Add yogurt, orange marmalade and vanilla, mix until combined.

3. Grease 12 individual silicone muffin tins, transfer cake batter into the prepared muffin tins.

4. Add 500ml water to pot. Push in the legs on the Cook & Crisp tray, then place the tray in the bottom position in the pot, place the muffin tins on the tray.

5. Close the lid and flip the SmartSwitch to RAPID COOKER. Select STEAM BAKE and set time to 30 minutes and temperature to 160° C. Select START/STOP to begin cooking. (until a knife inserted in the middle of the cakes comes out clean, if not, STEAM BAKE for another 5 minutes.)

6. When cooking is complete, open lid and remove from Speedi, brush with marmalade, leave to cool and serve.

Rhubarb Crumble

 Serving Size: 6

  Cooking Time: 35 Minutes

£ Cost Per Serving: 70p

INGREDIENTS

Filling
- 1 kg rhubarb, cut into 2 ½-cm pieces
- 200g caster sugar
- 30g plain flour
- 1 tsp vanilla essence

- 115g unsalted butter, softened
- 80g caster sugar

Topping:
- 120g plain flour

METHOD

1. In a bowl, add all filling ingredients and mix until combined. Set aside.

2. In another bowl, add all topping ingredients and rub with hands until resembles breadcrumbs.

3. Transfer the filling to 25 x 25-cm baking dish. Sprinkle the topping on the rhubarb.

4. Add 500ml water to pot. Push in the legs on the Cook & Crisp tray, then place the tray in the bottom position in the pot, place the baking dish on the tray.

5. Close the lid and flip the SmartSwitch to RAPID COOKER. Select STEAM BAKE and set time to 35 minutes and temperature to 180˚ C. Select START/STOP to begin cooking.

6. When cooking is complete, remove from Ninja Speedi and let cool for 30 minutes before

88

Rock Buns

 Yield: 12 Rock Buns  Cooking Time: 13 Minutes £ Cost Per Serving: 10p

INGREDIENTS

- 220g plain flour
- 1 ½ tsp baking powder
- Pinch of salt
- 90g unsalted butter
- 70g sugar
- 60g sultanas or mixed dried fruits
- 1 egg
- 70ml milk

METHOD

1. In a bowl, add flour, baking powder, salt. Mix until combined.

2. In another bowl, add the butter, sugar, egg and beat together until creamy. Add flour mixture and sultanas/dried fruits, mix with hands until combined. Do not over mix.

3. Push in the legs on the Cook & Crisp tray, then place the tray in the bottom position in the pot, line with baking paper. Place a tablespoon sized amount of dough (2-cm apart) on the lined tray.

4. Close the lid and flip the SmartSwitch to AIR FRY/HOB, then use the centre arrows to select BAKE/ROAST. Set temperature to 170˚ C and set time to 13 minutes. Select START/STOP to begin cooking.

5. When cooking is complete, remove from Ninja Speedi and serve warm.

Custard Creams

 *Yield:* 24 biscuits *Cooking Time:* 13 Minutes £ *Cost Per Serving:* 10p

INGREDIENTS

- 220g plain flour
- ¼ tsp bicarbonate of soda
- 220g unsalted butter, softened
- 90g icing sugar
- 100g No added sugar custard powder

- Filling
- 50g butter, softened
- 115g icing sugar
- a few drops of vanilla essence

METHOD

1. In a bowl, add the butter and icing sugar, beat until creamy, then add the flour, bicarbonate of soda, custard powder and mix until it forms a dough.

2. On a surface, roll the dough into a log and cut into 48 equal portions. Roll each portion into a ball and flatten slightly with a fork .

3. Push in the legs on the Cook & Crisp tray, then place the tray in the bottom position in the pot, line with baking paper. Place the biscuits on the lined tray.

4. Close the lid and flip the SmartSwitch to AIR FRY/HOB, then use the centre arrows to select BAKE/ROAST. Set temperature to 160˚ C and set time to 13 minutes. Select START/STOP to begin cooking.

5. When cooing is complete, remove from unit and set aside for 30 minutes to cool.

6. In a bowl, add the filling ingredients and beat until light and creamy. Spread the icing on each biscuit half (24 half) and sandwich together with remaining biscuits.

Scottish Tea Bread

 Yield: 1 loaf

 Cooking Time: 60 Minutes £ Cost Per Serving: 30p

INGREDIENTS

- 400g mixed dried fruit, soaked overnight in 300ml hot black tea and 150g brown sugar
- 1 egg, beaten
- 260g plain flour
- 130g unsalted butter, softened
- 2 tsp baking powder
- 1 tsp mixed spice

METHOD

1. Add flour, butter, mixed spices, baking powder and egg into the bowl of soaked mixed fruit. Mix until combined.

2. Grease 900g/2lb loaf tin. Pour the bread mixture into the loaf tin.

3. Push in the legs on the Cook & Crisp tray, then place the tray in the bottom position in the pot. Place the loaf on the tray.

4. Close the lid and flip the SmartSwitch to AIR FRY/HOB, then use the centre arrows to select BAKE/ROAST. Set temperature to 170° C and set time to 55 minutes, until a knife inserted in the middle comes out clean. Select START/STOP to begin cooking.

5. When cooing is complete, remove from Ninja Speedi and cool completely before slicing. Serve with a cup of tea.

Cream Buns

 *Yield: 6 Buns*    *Cooking Time: 25 Minutes*   £ *Cost Per Serving: 28p*

INGREDIENTS

- 300g plain flour
- Pinch of salt
- 2 tsp dried yeast
- 55g caster sugar, divided
- 190ml warm milk
- 60g soft butter

For the egg wash:
- 1 egg, beaten with 1 tbsp milk

For the filling:
- Icing sugar
- 240ml double cream, whipped
- 50g rasberry jam

METHOD

1. In a bowl, add the warm milk, yeast and ½ tsp of sugar. Allow to rest for a few minutes, until foamy.

2. Add the flour, salt, remaining sugar into the milk/yeast mixture and mix until combined. Add the softened butter while kneading until all the butter incorporated into the dough.

3. Cover the dough with a cling film. Leave in somewhere warm until the dough has doubled in size.After it's doubled in size, punch down the dough. Cut into 6 equal pieces shape into balls.

4. Push in the legs on the Cook & Crisp tray, then place the tray in the bottom position in the pot, line with baking paper. Place the buns (spaced apart) on the lined tray. Close the lid and leave for 30 minutes, until risen slightly.

5. Open lid, brush with egg wash.

6. Close the lid and flip the SmartSwitch to AIR FRY/HOB, then use the centre arrows to select BAKE/ROAST. Set temperature to 165˚ C and set time to 25 minutes. Select START/STOP to begin cooking.

7. When cooking is complete, remove from Ninja Speedi and cool completely.
Cut bun in half but leave the end intact, spread the jam on one side of the bun, then fill with whipped cream and sprinkle with icing sugar. Serve.

Shortbread

 **Yield:** *12 Shortbreads* **Cooking Time:** *15 Minutes* **£** *Cost Per Serving:* **20p**

INGREDIENTS

- 340g plain flour
- 100g caster sugar
- 230g unsalted butter, room temperature and cut into cubes

METHOD

1. In a bowl, add all ingredients and mix by hands until all combined. Do Not Over Mix.

2. Grease 20 x 20-cm baking tin. Press the dough into the tin, press and smooth surface. Use a knife to cut the dough into fingers, then pierce with a fork.

3. Push in the legs on the Cook & Crisp tray, then place the tray in the bottom position in the pot. Place the tin on the tray.

4. Close the lid and flip the SmartSwitch to AIR FRY/HOB, then use the centre arrows to select BAKE/ROAST. Set temperature to 170˚ C and set time to 15 minutes. Select START/STOP to begin cooking.

5. When cooking is complete, let cool in the tin before moving to rack to cool completely.

Jam and Coconut Cake

 *Yield:* 8 Buns　　 *Cooking Time:* 35 Minutes　　£ *Cost Per Serving:* 30p

INGREDIENTS

- 230g butter, softened
- 230g caster sugar
- 230g plain flour
- 1 tsp baking powder
- ½ tsp bicarbonate of soda
- 4 medium eggs (at room temperature)

- 200g Jam (raspberry, strawberry or blueberry)
- Handful desiccated coconut

METHOD

1. In a bowl, add flour, baking powder, bicarbonate of soda. Mix until combined.

2. In another bowl, add the butter, sugar and beat together until creamy. Add one egg at a time while beating, beat until combined. Add the flour mixture and fold it in gently with a wooden spoon, until combined.

3. Grease Multi-Purpose Tin or 20-cm cake tin and line with baking paper, transfer cake batter into the prepared tin.

4. Add 500ml water to pot. Push in the legs on the Cook & Crisp tray, then place the tray in the bottom position in the pot.

5. Close the lid and flip the SmartSwitch to RAPID COOKER. Select STEAM BAKE and set time to 35 minutes and temperature to 160˚ C. Select START/STOP to begin cooking.

6. When cooking is complete, remove the cake tin from Speedi and let cool slightly, then spread the cake top with jam and sprinkle with desiccated coconut.
Let cool completely. Slice and serve.

94

An old cake recipe that takes us back to our school days. Try this quick and simple jam and coconut cake. Warm custard on the side!

Victoria Loaf Cake

 *Serving Size:* 8    *Cooking Time:* 50 Minutes   £ *Cost Per Serving:* 52p

INGREDIENTS

Cake :

- 220g butter, softened
- 220g caster sugar
- 4 medium eggs
- 220g self-raising flour
- 1 tbsp milk, if needed
- 1 tsp vanilla essence

Filling:

- 300ml double cream, whipped
- 200g strawberry, hulled and sliced and mixed with 2 tbsp caster sugar

METHOD

1. In a bowl, add butter and sugar. Beat until creamy, add vanilla and eggs one at a time while beating. Add the flour to the butter mixture gradually while beating until combined. (if you find the batter is thick add 1 tbsp milk).

2. Grease 2lb loaf tin, transfer the cake batter into the greased loaf tin.

3. Pour 250ml water into the pot. Push in the legs on the Cook & Crisp tray, then place the tray in the bottom position in the pot. Add loaf tin on the tray.

4. Close the lid and flip the SmartSwitch to RAPID COOKER. Select STEAM BAKE, set temperature to 160˚ C and set time to 50 minutes. Select START/STOP to begin cooking.

5. When cooking is complete, open the lid and check the cake is ready by inserting a skewer into the centre. If it comes out clean, remove the cake from the Ninja Speedi and cool completely on a wire rack. If not, bake for another 3 minutes before testing again with a skewer.

6. When ready to serve, slice cake in half fill with double cream and strawberries.

Peanut Butter Biscuits

Serving Size: 24 Biscuits

Cooking Time: 10 Minutes

Cost Per Serving: 27p

INGREDIENTS

- 190g plain flour
- 3/4 tsp bicarbonate of soda
- ½ tsp baking powder
- 115g unsalted butter, softened
- 100g caster sugar
- 80g light soft brown sugar
- 190g smooth peanut butter
- 1 large egg
- 1 ½ tsp vanilla essence
- Pinch of salt

METHOD

1. In a bowl, add flour, baking powder, bicarbonate of soda, salt. Mix until combined.

2. In another bowl, add the butter, sugar and beat together until creamy. Add egg and vanilla while beating, then add the peanut butter and beat until combined.

3. Add the flour, mixture and mix by hand until combined.

4. Line the Cook & Crisp tray with baking paper.Push in the legs on the Cook & Crisp tray, then place the tray in the bottom position in the pot.

5. Form dough into balls (2 tablespoon of dough for each ball). Place on the tray and flatten slightly with a fork. (You`ll need to work in batches).

6. Close the lid and flip the SmartSwitch to AIR FRY/HOB, then use the centre arrows to select BAKE/ROAST. Set temperature to 165° C and set time to 10 minutes. Select START/STOP to begin cooking.

7. When cooking is complete, open lid and let cool on the tray for 5 minutes then transfer to a wire rack to cool completely.

97

Hot Cross Buns

Serving Size: 8 Buns   *Cooking Time:* 25 Minutes   £ *Cost Per Serving:* 25p

INGREDIENTS

- 500g plain flour, divided
- 100g caster sugar, divided
- 70g melted unsalted butter
- 1 tsp salt
- 180ml warm milk
- 2 large egg, beaten
- 1 tsp ground cinnamon
- 1 tsp ground nutmeg
- 150g raisins
- 2 ¼ tsp dried yeast

For the cross:
- 75g plain flour mixed with 6 tbsp water

For glazing:
- Golden syrup

METHOD

1. In a bowl, add milk, melted butter and eggs. Mix.

2. In another bowl, add flour, sugar, yeast, salt, cinnamon, nutmeg, raisins. Mix.

3. Add the milk mixture into the flour mixture and knead until combined. Continue to knead for 3 more minutes. Dough will be a little sticky and soft. Let the dough in the bowl and cover until it doubled in size.

4. Punch the dough down to release the air. Divide dough into 8 pieces. Roll them into 8 balls.

5. Line the Cook & Crisp tray with baking paper. Add 500ml water into the Ninja Speedi pot. Push in the legs on the Cook & Crisp tray, then place the tray in the bottom position in the pot. Place the buns on the tray. Close the lid and leave to prove for 30 minutes.

6. After 30 minutes, pipe a cross on each bun with the flour/water mixture.

7. Close the lid and flip the SmartSwitch to RAPID COOKER. Select STEAM BAKE, set temperature to 180° C and set time to 25 minutes. Select START/STOP to begin cooking.

8. When cooking is complete, open lid and let cool for 5 minutes then then brush with golden syrup. Serve.

98

Strawberry Tea Cake

 *Serving Size:* **6**    *Cooking Time:* **13 Minutes**   £ *Cost Per Serving:* **60p**

INGREDIENTS

Cake:
- 115g unsalted butter, soft
- 240g self-raising flour
- 1 tsp baking powder
- 200g caster sugar
- 240ml milk
- 4 eggs
- 1 tsp vanilla

Strawberry and Cream:
- 350g strawberries, hulled and sliced
- 50g caster sugar
- 200ml double cream, whisked until thick
- 1 tsp vanilla essence

METHOD

1. In a large bowl, add the sliced strawberries, sugar. Mash slightly with a fork, cover and set aside.

2. In a bowl, add butter and sugar. Beat until creamy, add vanilla and eggs, milk while beating. Add the flour, baking powder to the butter mixture gradually while beating until combined.

3. Transfer batter into a greased 20-cm cake tin.

4. Add 500ml water into the Ninja Speedi pot. Push in the legs on the Cook & Crisp tray, then place the tray in the bottom position in the pot. Place the tin on the tray.

5. Close the lid and flip the SmartSwitch to RAPID COOKER. Select STEAM BAKE, set temperature to 160° C and set time to 13 minutes. Select START/STOP to begin cooking.

6. When cooking is complete, open lid and remove from Ninja Speedi. Allow the cake to cool for 10 mins. Remove from tin, transfer to a cooling rack. Top with strawberry mixture and cream, slice and serve with tea.

Raisin Loaf

 **Serving Size:** *12*    **Cooking Time:** *25 Minutes*   £ **Cost Per Serving:** *20p*

INGREDIENTS

- 100g raisins and currants soaked in 360ml hot water for 2 hours
- 1 ½ tsp dried yeast
- 240ml warm water
- 200g plain flour
- 2 tbsp softened butter

METHOD

1. Drain raisins and currants, reserving 120ml of soaking liquid.

2. In a bowl, add water and sprinkle with yeast, set aside for 10 minutes.

3. In a bowl, add flour and butter, rub with hands until combined. Add yeast mixture and the 120ml reserved liquid, knead until combined. Add raisins, currants, knead for 3 minutes.

4. Form into a ball. Transfer to a bowl, cover with a towel, and let rise in a warm place until doubled in size.

5. Grease two 1lb loaf tins. Form dough into two loaf shapes and place into loaf tins. Sprinkle with flour, cover with towel, and let rise until reaches top of tins.

6. Add 500ml water into the Ninja Speedi pot. Push in the legs on the Cook & Crisp tray, then place the tray in the bottom position in the pot. Place the tins on the tray.

7. Close the lid and flip the SmartSwitch to RAPID COOKER. Select STEAM BAKE, set temperature to 180° C and set time to 25 minutes. Select START/STOP to begin cooking.

8. When cooking complete, open lid and remove the loaf tins. Let cool completely on a wire rack before slicing and serving.

INDEX

Afternoon Tea

Printed in Great Britain
by Amazon

25101795R00057